CONFESSIONS OF A HIGH SCHOOL WORD NERD

Increase Your SAT Verbal Score
While Laughing Your **Gluteus**✱ Off

EDITED BY

ARIANNE COHEN AND COLLEEN KINDER

PENGUIN BOOKS

PENGUIN BOOKS
Published by the Penguin Group
Penguin Group (USA) Inc.,
375 Hudson Street, New York, New York 10014, U.S.A.
Penguin Group (Canada), 90 Eglinton Avenue East, Suite 700, Toronto,
Ontario, Canada M4P 2Y3
(a division of Pearson Penguin Canada Inc.)
Penguin Books Ltd, 80 Strand, London WC2R 0RL, England
Penguin Ireland, 25 St Stephen's Green, Dublin 2, Ireland
(a division of Penguin Books Ltd)
Penguin Group (Australia), 250 Camberwell Road, Camberwell, Victoria 3124, Australia
(a division of Pearson Australia Group Pty Ltd)
Penguin Books India Pvt Ltd, 11 Community Centre, Panchsheel Park,
New Delhi–110 017, India
Penguin Group (NZ), cnr Airborne and Rosedale Roads, Albany,
Auckland 1310, New Zealand
(a division of Pearson New Zealand Ltd.)
Penguin Books (South Africa) (Pty) Ltd, 24 Sturdee Avenue, Rosebank,
Johannesburg 2196, South Africa

Penguin Books Ltd, Registered Offices:
80 Strand, London WC2R 0RL, England

First published in Penguin Books 2006

1 3 5 7 9 10 8 6 4 2

Page 207 constitutes an extension of this copyright page.

Definitions from *The Penguin Webster Handy College Dictionary*, third edition, 2003; The Merriam-Webster Online Dictionary; *The Random House Unabridged Dictionary*, 2005; *The American Heritage Dictionary of the English Language*, fourth edition, 2006; *Webster's Revised Unabridged Dictionary*, 1996, 1998; Webster's *New Millennium Dictionary of English*, preview edition, 2003–2005.

LIBRARY OF CONGRESS CATALOGING IN PUBLICATION DATA
Confessions of a high school word nerd : increase your SAT verbal score while laughing
your gluteus★ off/edited by Arianne Cohen & Colleen Kinder.—1st ed.
p. cm.
ISBN 978-0-14-303836-8
1. SAT (Educational test)—Study guides.   I. Cohen, Arianne.
II. Kinder, Colleen.   III. Title.
LB2353.57.C66 2007
378.1'662—dc22   2006029620

Printed in the United States of America
Set in Bembo • Designed by Ginger Legato

To Kate Storey and Richard Mitchell at Holy Angels Academy, Judy Krouse at Germantown Academy, and all of the high school teachers who make big words palatable.

CONTENTS

INTRODUCTION

So you're buckling down to study for the SAT. You've got your fat book of practice tests on one side, and on the other, a heap of flashcards of words that you don't know. But there's a problem. Two problems, actually. You soon discover that "practice test" is a fancy term for self-torture, and as you flip through your alphabetized vocabulary cards, all the words start to look exactly the same: BIG.

This book is the solution to your attempts to study-but-not-*really*-study. We've taken all of the **S**uffering, **A**ngst, and **T**orture out of the **SAT**. In the pages ahead, you'll find hilarious stories about high school life, sprinkled with the language you need to ace the SAT. Our wild tales of sports games, first kisses, and senior pranks also helpfully include vocabulary in bold. With all of the definitions footnoted right below, you won't have to lift a finger to learn.

The young people who wrote these stories know what it's like to be in high school. They also know how to laugh about it and tell a damn good story. Take Dave, for example. Dave helped **execute** the best senior prank in his high school's history by filling his school lobby with squealing pigs. Or Laure,

---

Execute: v. to do; perform; carry out.

who decided to **expedite** her first kiss by calling a boy in her class and asking him if he wanted to smooch.

Sound too good to count as studying? The authors of this book are so smart that they've taken all the work out of test prep! As you read ahead, you'll also sit shotgun with Colleen while she fails her first (and second) road test and nearly runs over her English teacher. You'll get to watch Chris mastermind (well, sort of) a band-camp water-balloon massacre, volunteer with Kara as one of her mental-hospital patients escapes, and run alongside Lauren as she pursues her nemesis on the soccer field. And visiting Arianne, you'll find out what it's like to be **evicted** from multiple homes (Yes, that means "kicked out").

We were all in your shoes just a few years ago. We wrote this book to make you laugh about the silly drama and wild memories of high school, *and* to prepare you for the SAT. By the time you're done **perusing** this book, you'll know those SAT words cold, and ace the test. But if you laugh half as hard as we did, you won't even notice that you're learning.

Expedite: v. to quicken the progress of.
Evict: v. to expel; dispossess.
Peruse: v. to read attentively.

CONFESSIONS OF A HIGH SCHOOL WORD NERD

1

CONFESSIONS OF A DILIGENT KISSER

Laure de Vulpillieres

Why did kissing Chris seem like a good idea? To understand that, you need to know about my biggest high school **insecurity**: I was not particularly **feminine**. My whole life, I've been a tomboy to the core, **spurning** dresses and cute shoes, and embracing pants and sneakers instead. Flower prints still make me gag.

Before adolescence, I was **content** being a tomboy. But when I hit the teenage years, I saw that my friends were turning into attractive women, and I was becoming, um . . . well, I wasn't sure what I was becoming. My insecurities grew, **culminating** in a roar of peer pressure that made me determined to prove my femininity. To begin, I tried dressing like a ravishing **vixen**. I grew my hair long, wore flower prints, and **dabbled** in the world of **ostentatious** jewelry. I looked like a **displaced** hippie.

Insecurity: n. self-doubt; something unstable.
Feminine: adj. relating to, or like, woman.
Spurn: v. to reject with disdain.
Content: adj. satisfied; easy in mind.
Culminate: v. to reach the highest point.
Vixen: n. a sexually attractive woman.
Dabble: v. to do anything in a superficial manner.
Ostentatious: adj. pretentiously displayed.
Displace: v. to put out of the usual or proper place.

1

Thus began my plot to kiss Chris.

My school was in the French countryside, where girls are even more girly than they are in America. My dad is French, and I grew up near Paris before moving to the United States for college. In case you're curious, kids from France have all the same hang-ups as American high schoolers—they just complain about them in a different language, while eating **bizarre** foods.

Our high school was not **dissimilar** to yours. It always seemed like everyone was making out with each other. In actuality, only a handful of people were making out, and they were just talking about it **bombastically**. Those who weren't making out would just fancifully **exaggerate** the stories of those who were. High school, after all, was all about **hyperbole**. At the time, I **stationed** myself among the best of the **gossipmongers**, where it really did seem like every single female but me had established her **credibility** by making out with a boy.

So I decided to do the same. **Luring** a guy to my lips would **validate** my attractiveness. Once I had smooched, I would be **indelibly** marked as feminine in the eyes of the world (*ahem*, the school). Perfect.

Bizarre: adj. odd; whimsical; grotesque.
Dissimilar: adj. unlike.
Bombastic: adj. pompous; overblown.
Exaggerate: v. to represent as large, important, etc., beyond the truth; magnify falsely.
Hyperbole: n. obvious exaggeration; an extravagant statement.
Station: v. to assign; place.
Gossipmonger: n. a person who starts or spreads gossip.
Credibility: n. the quality or power of inspiring belief.
Lure: v. to entice.
Validate: v. to make valid; to confirm.
Indelible: adj. not capable of being deleted or obliterated.

Chris sat in front of me in class, which gave me **ample** opportunity to stare at the back of his head and think up a plan. From behind, I had a clear view of his back arched over his desk, kind of like l'Arc de Triomphe, but covered by a blue T-shirt and longish brown hair. Chris was one of those average guys with average features and average **charisma**, not to mention average personality and average intelligence. His one **exceptional** skill was the ability to draw **negligible** attention to himself. I may have been the only person in the school to have ever stared at him.

Chris was not the kind of guy you would write **amorous** notes to, and for this reason, Chris was perfect for my purposes. I began scheming a "Kiss Plan," while mopeding to school (French kids are allowed to moped), smoking during lunch break (French kids are allowed to smoke), and while mopeding home. I was pondering the Plan one evening when I came home and dropped my bag in the front entryway, **wilting** into a chair at the kitchen table. I heard my mom walk down the hall toward the kitchen.

My mom's footsteps **distinguished** themselves from any other family member's because of their **uniquely** slow pace. My mom was sick with breast cancer and had been since I was ten. She was fighting the cancer with all her might. While she managed to live for another nine years, some days could be

Ample: adj. plentiful; sufficient.
Charisma: n. a power for eliciting enthusiastic popular support attributed to a person or position.
Exceptional: adj. unusual; extraordinary.
Negligible: adj. of little importance.
Amorous: adj. inclined to love; loving.
Wilt: v. to become or make limp or drooping.
Distinguish: v. to mark, recognize, or see as distinct or different.
Unique: adj. being the only one of its kind; unusual; rare.

really **grueling** for her. My mom had come into the kitchen to take her evening dose of vitamins and medicine, and as she counted out pills on the table, she asked how I was.

I didn't really want to discuss the Kiss Plan with my mother. Even she had been cool enough as a high schooler to kiss all the boys. There is nothing worse than being less cool than one's own mother. I shrugged **noncommittally** and changed the subject to my brother.

"I'm fine. Where's Benjamin?" I took a sip of my milk, a much fattier version of what people drink in America.

My mom rolled her eyes. "If only we could tie him down! Then at least we'd know where he was. Maybe he's stealing the neighbor's goat again . . ."

The milk squirted out my nose as I laughed, and my mother handed me a napkin. When my brother was little, his favorite game was called "Where's Benjamin?" He would hide in a room and my parents would **prowl** around **dramatically**, looking under couches and lifting up pillows, trying to find him. It seemed that he never outgrew that game, because now, at seventeen, he would **amble** off outside, wander into the basement, or **evaporate** right as the table needed to be cleared. In one particularly memorable disappearance, he'd reappeared hours later with the neighbor's goat.

My dad found Benjamin's disappearances **infuriating**. He would try to yell at Benjamin, but my brother was **incorrigible**.

Grueling: adj. exhausting; tiringly severe.
Noncommittal: adj. not committing oneself to a positive view or course.
Prowl: v. to roam about in search of something.
Dramatic: adj. pertaining to drama.
Amble: v. to move easily and gently, like a walking horse.
Evaporate: v. to disappear.
Infuriate: to make furious; enrage.
Incorrigible: adj. resistant to correction or reform; beyond reform.

And my dad, **fatigued** from his long days at work, wasn't very good at **upbraiding** him.

While my parents searched for Benjamin, I drank my milk and mentally **perused** the menfolk of my class. I had previously **pined** for a basketball player named Claude, but he seemed to be ignoring my flower prints and jewelry. And my friend Michael was friends with my brother, so that certainly wouldn't work. Chris continued to lead the pack of potential kissers, with one **elementary** quality that made him a prime **candidate**: He had never kissed anyone either.

Because flirting would take too long, I decided be more direct with Chris. Sometimes the best solutions are the simplest ones, and I figured I'd just ask him to kiss me (a strategy which, *ahem*, still works to this day). At the time, I was a **neophyte** in the art of **procuring** kisses, and had no idea what I was doing.

After dinner, my brother disappeared again, leaving a table of dirty dishes. My mom was safely out of earshot, so I picked up the phone and called Chris. When he answered, I panicked and took the **cowardly** path:

"Er, sorry Chris, what was the history homework for this week?"

Except I was speaking in French, so it was more like:

Fatigue: n. weariness from physical or mental exertion.
Upbraid: v. to blame; rebuke.
Peruse: to examine or consider with attention and in detail.
Pine: v. to long (for).
Elementary: adj. simple; pertaining to basic facts.
Candidate: n. one who seeks an office or honor.
Neophyte: n. a beginner; novice.
Procure: v. to obtain.
Cowardly: adj. shrinking from pain or danger.

"Er, excuse-moi Chris, mais est-ce que tu sais ce qu'on doit faire en histoire pour cette semaine?"

My knees shook as he answered my query.

"Read chapter six."

I thanked him and hung up.

Ugh. I was the lamest high schooler alive. How could I look at anyone ever again? I couldn't even ask a guy to kiss me. But, as my mother had taught me over the past half decade, when you fall off the horse, you need to get right back on. So before I could **agonize** about it further, I dialed Chris's number again. He answered—again.

"Sorry, Chris. There was a real reason that I called." I dove right in. "Um, do you think that you and I could kiss sometime?"

There—I said it! My request was **gauche**, but now it was out in the open. I could only wait for his response.

Silence. Chris thought about it. I waited. My knees shook. Ten seconds passed.

More silence. For the first time, it occurred to me that my kiss request could be denied.

"Yeah, OK," Chris said.

Phew! I **crumbled** to the floor with the phone still in my hand. Chris went on to remark that I had an oddly **straightforward** approach. Then we tried to figure out the details of our Plan. When should the kiss happen? We **conspired** to hang out together over lunch the next day.

After a night of **insomnia**, I awoke to **don** my most vixenlike

Agonize: v. to suffer anguish; to distress; to put forth great effort.
Gauche: adj. socially awkward.
Crumble: v. to break into small pieces; disintegrate.
Straightforward: adj. direct.
Conspire: v. to plot secretly with another person.
Insomnia: n. the inability to sleep.
Don: v. to put on.

outfit: a pink-skirt-with-black-top combo that my mother had bought me. I mopeded to school a half hour early and watched the clock—and Chris's back—through morning classes, feeling totally **preoccupied**. When the bell rang, I followed Chris out of class and down the stairs to the exit, our eyes **anxiously** lowered to our feet. We tried to look **nonchalant** as we trotted into the woods nearby.

Dang, I was so nervous. So was he. We sat on a log bench and awkwardly conversed about school—upcoming homework, spring vacation plans, sports teams—all while sitting a yard apart, distracted by the task that lay ahead. At a couple points we scooted toward each other, but the notion of approaching each other's heads seemed so awkward that it **stymied** our progress even more. **Laboriously**, we repeated our conversation **cycle**, returning to the topic of homework.

A ringing bell echoed into the woods.

Defeated, we got up and returned to school. Our lips had not touched.

But I'm no quitter. I decided that what we needed was a **catalyst**—an excuse to get close. I envisioned a **monsoon** tearing through school and Chris lifting me through the window to safety, holding me tenderly in his arms, then leaning down to kiss me. . . .

No, that would never happen. Chris couldn't even lift me.

What normal couples' activities could I organize? Bowling?

Preoccupy: v. to take the attention of, to the exclusion of other matters.
Anxious: adj. full of anxiety; worried.
Nonchalant: adj. full of disinterest; coolly unconcerned.
Stymied: adj. blocked by a minor but insurmountable obstacle.
Laborious: adj. not easy; requiring much work or exertion.
Cycle: n. a series or round.
Catalyst: n. the person or thing that sets off or causes an event.
Monsoon: n. the seasonal wind, or the rainy season, of South Asia.

No, bowling is a noncontact activity. Maybe dancing? A dance would be an **opportune** situation for Chris and I to stand together. Yes, a romantic song would unleash my inner vixen, providing the ideal conditions for that lip-lock.

Since no one I knew would be hosting any parties in the **foreseeable** future, the **onus** was on me to host one. The added bonus of kissing at a dance would be an audience—just the public **validation** I needed. Awesome.

With my parents' permission, I kicked into dance-planning mode. I invited cool classmates, cleaned out the big room in the basement, and even mowed the lawn. My mom lay on the couch, temporarily on bed rest from chemotherapy, watching me zoom back and forth across the house. She joked that I should have parties more often if it meant cleaning the house so **zealously**.

The big day arrived. Friends and classmates flowed into my streamer-**adorned** basement, with girls moving off to **twitter** in one corner and boys grouping together to stare at their shoes in another corner. This sex segregation is the **status quo** for any teenage dance, so I felt calm. I waited for Chris, hoping he was still onboard with the Kiss Plan.

Fortunately, Chris was just as anxious to lose his lip virginity, and had **adroitly** convinced his parents to drive the hourlong **expanse** from his home to mine. I opened my front door to see Chris—and his mother. Chris explained that because of

Opportune: adj. timely; appropriate.
Foresee: v. to predict; anticipate.
Onus: n. a burden; a charge.
Validation: n. an act, process, or instance of confirming.
Zealous: adj. earnest; ardently active; devoted.
Adorn: v. to decorate; dress with ornaments; embellish.
Twitter: v. to giggle.
Status quo: n. the existing state or condition.
Adroit: adj. expert in the use of hands or body; skillful; ingenious.
Expanse: n. an uninterrupted stretch or area.

the distance between our houses, his mom preferred to wait in the living room with a book until the party ended. I stuck my head into my mom's bedroom to **notify** her of the overage company.

Well, at least Chris is here, I thought. As long as his mom didn't dance with us, this arrangement would do. My mom **hobbled** to the door and greeted Chris's mom warmly, happy to have another adult in the house while teenagers overran the basement and leaked out into the garden.

French teenagers prefer slow music because the **measured** beats give girls and boys an excuse to be close to one another. More importantly, slow music is easy to dance to. French teens aren't **audacious** like American high schoolers who groove to rap and hip-hop. All French fifteen-year-olds know that no matter how motor challenged they are, they can master the **deliberate** rocking from one foot to another, hands on their partners' waists or shoulders, turning in slow circles.

Chris and I couldn't waste any more time. We walked directly onto the dance floor, still not comfortable enough to hold hands. **Eschewing** small talk, we skipped right to the moment of truth. The song changed to "November Rain" by Guns N' Roses, which runs a blessed ten minutes. We would need at least that long.

As Chris and I rocked in slow circles, we moved closer to each other. Chris **hesitantly** touched my hip, and I reached up to put two hands on his shoulders. He moved closer and closer

---

Notify: v. to give attention to; inform.
Hobble: v. to limp; proceed haltingly.
Measured: adj. regular; deliberate.
Audacious: adj. bold; daring; intrepid.
Deliberate: adj. intentional.
Eschew: v. to keep away from; avoid.
Hesitant: adj. hesitating or prone to hesitation; undecided.

until I could feel his breath on my ear. His cheek was next to mine. I realized that he would need to pull back a little if our lips were going to meet. For the first time, Chris and I were *too* close for kissing.

About three minutes into the song, he awkwardly pulled away from me and made the move. Finally, his lips met mine. Thank heavens.

My first thought? His lips are cold.

Soon thereafter, his tongue got involved. This truly caught me by surprise. (Despite the name, French kissing is not a particularly French habit.) I had never thought about the **mechanics** of kissing, and had assumed it would be a dry experience. This kiss was not an **arid** one.

I became aware of folks watching us. The audience that I was eagerly **anticipating** turned out to be a massive one. I realized that if I was looking at the onlookers, this meant I was probably kissing Chris bug-eyed. So I reminded myself to shut my eyes. The song rolled into its **finale**, and we ducked out of the room, holding hands at last. As Chris led me upstairs, I **subtly** dried my mouth with my free hand. I couldn't stop grinning.

At the end of the night, we had to separate his mom and mine. They now appeared to be Best Friends Forever. They didn't seem to notice that their children had matured in the **intervening** hours. His mother looked at her watch and gasped

---

Mechanics: n. functional details or procedure.
Arid: adj. lacking moisture; parched with heat.
Anticipate: v. to expect; foresee.
Finale: n. a closing scene, especially of a musical performance.
Subtle: adj. artful; crafty.
Intervene: v. to happen between things, persons, or events.

at the time, briefly lecturing Chris about bedtime. He stared at his feet, **mortified**. I winked at him, and then went to turn off the music downstairs and **bid** my guests adieu.

As classmates **meandered** off to their parents' cars, my dad pulled into the driveway, ragged from a long Friday at the office, and stood his briefcase on the kitchen counter. My mom **shuffled** into the kitchen behind him. Miraculously, my brother happened to blow into the kitchen as well, hiding his head behind the refrigerator door.

While my mom settled herself on a cushioned stool, my dad asked me how the party had gone.

"The party was perfect, Dad. It was exactly what I needed."

By the time I answered, my brother had already disappeared for the night.

My mom wanted details, eager to know if "any romances had bloomed downstairs." Good old mom. I humored her with a **plethora** of stories about the party, but nothing about Chris. Though the Kiss Plan had succeeded, I was still too embarrassed to admit the details to anyone (except all of you). I never did tell her.

The following Monday, when Chris and I crossed paths in the hall, we avoided eye contact, as we would for the next two years. The gossipmongers of our high school went ahead and **extrapolated** a **sordid** drama between us—*He cheated on her! And then she dumped him! And they swore never to speak ever again!*—but the truth was, our mission was simply accomplished.

Mortify: v. to humiliate.
Bid: v. to command; invite; give expression to.
Meander: v. to wander aimlessly; persue a winding course.
Shuffle: v. to move with scraping feet.
Plethora: n. an overfullness; superabundance.
Extrapolate: v. to project on the basis of known data; infer.
Sordid: adj. base; vile; dirty.

❋ **Laure de Vulpillieres** grew up in a village outside of Paris, France, where though her kissing options were limited, the cows and wheat stalks were plentiful. She attended Harvard University, and lives in Phnom Penh, Cambodia, working as a consultant for humanitarian organizations. She still does not like dresses, and can say so in English, French, and now in Cambodian.

2

CONFESSIONS OF A REBEL TROMBONIST

Chris Heaney

As an eighth-grader on the brink of high school, I doubted that marching band was a "cool" thing to do. In fact, joining the band seemed more like social suicide. If I had any desire for a normal weekend life, with **convivial** parties and maybe a girlfriend to **accompany** me, then I should stay far, far away from the guys with the trombones.

But the "bandies" began recruiting us before we had even stepped foot in a high school class. I remember sitting on the aluminum bleachers of the football field with the rest of my eighth-grade class, as the band put on their show. The high school building lay just beyond the end zone, and I couldn't even **fathom** what life was like inside its red-brick walls. I hoped it had a lot to do with chemistry lab explosions and sexily **indiscreet** cheerleaders. But before I could get carried away with these fantasies, the marching band began charging across the football field.

Convivial: adj. festive; agreeable; jovial.
Accompany: v. to go with; be associated with.
Fathom: v. to penetrate and come to understand.
Indiscreet: adj. lacking in judgment.

It was a **comical** sight. They were dressed like **festive** toy soldiers and clutched their instruments like rifles. Their maroon jackets bore gold **epaulets** and white embroidery. Their pants were white with gold racing stripes—way too baggy for most band members and too small for the rest. Worst of all, each band member had a **massive** plume of white feathers sprouting from his hat.

The marching band's closest equivalent to "hot cheerleaders" was the "color guard" girls, who wore purple boas. They waved **diaphanous** pink flags in the sun while the rest of the band blared **euphonious** music at us. Watching from a top bleacher, I could make little sense of the **convoluted** formations the band marched in. Then, **abruptly**, the band stopped dead in their tracks and almost blew the bleachers over with one final blast of sound. This was the **zenith** of the performance and every bandy was out of breath by its end.

A grin spread across my face. At age thirteen, I was a dork myself: short, **corpulent**, with a mop of brown hair I had **emulated** from a poster of the Beatles. I was a bookworm from birth, with enough **erudition** to annoy both my classmates *and* my teachers. And I didn't even play a cool instrument. If I was

Comical: adj. droll; funny; exciting mirth.
Festive: adj. joyous; relating to a feast or holiday.
Epaulet: n. a decoration on the shoulder of a jacket, especially on a military uniform.
Massive: adj. bulky; heavy.
Diaphanous: adj. transparent or transluscent.
Euphonious: adj. having a pleasant sound.
Convoluted: adj. too complex or intricate to understand easily.
Abrupt: adj. beginning, ending, or changing suddenly or with a break.
Zenith: n. the highest point of anything; culmination.
Corpulent: adj. bulky of body; stout; fat.
Emulate: v. to strive to equal or excel; to imitate with effort to surpass.
Erudition: n. knowledge acquired through study and reading.

going to be a musical **novice**, I could have at least chosen the drums and joined some garage rock band. Instead, I had chosen the trombone, making myself a **vulnerable** target for the marching-band recruiter: the **infamous** Mr. G.

He stood before us on the lowest bleacher. Unlike the sports coaches that led practices in sweatpants, Mr. G. was dressed **immaculately** in **formal** black slacks and a crisp white dress shirt. Even his shoes shone. He had curly reddish-blond hair, a pale complexion, and aviator sunglasses perched on his nose.

"My name . . . is Mr. G." There was a pause in his **oration**, as if he expected applause from us. "I am . . . the band director. You have just watched the product of three intense months of physical, mental, and musical training."

The cooler eighth-graders tried to **suppress** their giggles. He went on, **pontificating** about the value of the band: friendship, school pride, and leadership skills. It sounded like he was giving us the script of our college essays. But no one felt very **edified** by his speech.

Sensing that our interest was **waning**, Mr. G. yelled, "And I haven't even told you about . . . BAND CAMP!"

Novice: n. a person who is new to the circumstances in which he or she is placed.

Vulnerable: adj. susceptible of being assaulted or conquered; open to attack.

Infamous: adj. notoriously evil; shamefully bad; wicked.

Immaculate: adj. perfectly clean; spotless.

Formal: adj. adhering to established form or mode; conventional; ceremonious.

Oration: n. a formal and dignified public speech.

Suppress: v. to restrain; abolish.

Pontificate: v. to speak about something in a knowing and pompous way, especially when not qualified to do so.

Edify: v. to instruct and improve, especially in moral and religious knowledge.

Wane: v. to decrease, as in size; decline.

There was silence, and not the good kind. I could hear the crickets in the field behind us.

Mr. G. motioned to a tall redhead. "Brian's here to tell you more about it."

Brian stepped forward. Somehow, he managed to look **suave** despite being dressed like the Nutcracker.

"So, yeah, band camp . . ." he began, in that **nonchalant** tone that sounds cool in any teenager's ears. The eighth-grade girls held their breath. ". . . It rocks. We get to play all day, raid the girls' cabins, and"—Brian finally smiled—"there's a massive water-balloon fight each year. Everyone gets wet. But Mr. G. gets SOAKED."

"OK, Brian, that's enough," Mr. G. cut his spokesman off.

But the damage was done. Giggles rippled through the bleachers. Brian's **depiction** sounded like the water-balloon fight of every teenager's dreams. I could just picture the girls in wet T-shirts. Suddenly, band didn't seem so dorky anymore. In fact, camp sounded like a **superb** way to kick off high school—with some **chaos**, flirtation, and a whole lot of noise.

That August, a **missive** arrived in my mailbox demanding my presence in the high school parking lot at 6:30 A.M. the following Monday. Only when I read the packing list did I remember why I'd signed up for bandy boot camp. Underneath the words "sunblock," "bug spray," and "bathing suit," someone had scribbled "WATER BALLOONS" in red crayon. Oh yes.

So I prepared for Camp Bernie, throwing on my cherry-red Grateful Dead T-shirt. Even though the only Dead song I

Suave: adj. smooth in texture, performance, or style.
Nonchalant: adj. calm and unconcerned about matters.
Depiction: n. portrayal; representation by or as if by a picture.
Superb: adj. magnificent; elegant; excellent.
Chaos: n. the absence of form or order; utter confusion.
Missive: n. a letter or written communication.

knew was "Casey Jones," I pretended to like my shirt for the edgy, alternative look. In reality, I had never taken anything stronger than Tylenol in my entire life. But I knew it was important to put forth the right image in high school, and it was about time I looked cool.

I boarded the bus to Camp Bernie, hoping to sit next to my middle school crush: Eleni, a busty **coquette** with beautiful, curly black hair. As I walked toward her, she leapt up and spread her arms. I might be a **verbose** trombonist with glasses, I thought, but Eleni must be into that now!

"TIM!" she yelled.

"No, it's 'Chri—'" I began correcting, but she was already pushing past me to embrace a tan and muscular **ruffian** with a drumstick. He patted her head, making **ripplets** in her mass of hair.

"Hey, *gaaaww*-geous!" he said, his voice purring like a Porsche.

Tim. I **resented** him immediately. Tim was also a freshman, but because he had given up football for marching band, his coolness was guaranteed. He wore an earring, talked like a gangster, and gave everyone high fives. Tim, also known as T-Ros, looked positively **predatory** when he glanced at the ladies—like he could have his pick.

How was I going to **ascend** the marching-band totem

Coquette: n. a flirtatious woman.
Verbose: adj. wordy; containing more words than necessary.
Ruffian: n. someone who behaves in a rough, bullying, or violent way, often a member of a gang of criminal thugs.
Ripplet: n. a small ripple.
Resent: v. to be indignant at, as an insult; to show or feel displeasure from a sense of injury.
Predatory: adj. preying upon others; acting with selfish motives.
Ascend: v. to climb up something; to rise or lead to a higher level.

pole with Tim in my way? How would I **supplant** him—my **nemesis**—as the band's newest cool guy?

Two words: "water balloons."

❋

"THIS AFTERNOON! WATER-BALLOON FIGHT!" Brian, the field captain, yelled. He was trying to be **authoritative** around us newcomers, **clipping** his sentences like a **peremptory** boss.

"Your balloons! Don't forget them!" Brian said, softening his **officious** tone. "Or your game face!" This was the moment I had been waiting for.

After lunch, we disbanded as quickly as cockroaches and spent the next hour preparing for battle in our bunks. I filled a red balloon halfway, so that it was the size of an overripe tomato and could be **whanged** into Mr. G.'s face from afar. He'd never know who hit him! Then I filled one for Eleni: a yellow balloon about the size of a cantaloupe. I would **lob** it through the air and leave her sopping wet. Yes, this was my idea of flirting. Lastly, I filled an industrial-strength helium balloon until it looked like a watermelon. This one would be dropped from the roof—onto Tim's head.

Supplant: v. to displace and take the place of.

Nemesis: n. a formidable rival or opponent.

Authoritative: adj. having due authority; showing an expectation of being obeyed.

Clip: v. to cut, as with shears; truncate.

Peremptory: adj. putting an end to an action or debate.

Officious: adj. acting unduly important; aggressive in offering unrequested help.

Whang: v. to hit something and produce a loud resounding sound.

Lob: v. to strike or toss something so that is moves slowly through the air in a high arc.

Before we could begin hurling our water rockets at each other, Mr. G. stepped forward. "I'm only going to say this once, so listen up," he said. "If anyone hits me with a water balloon when I'm not holding the flag, I will destroy them." Mr. G. looked serious, but we had all heard his **redundant** warnings and had tuned them out long ago.

When he blew the whistle, we began our **orgy** of flying latex and cold splashes of water. Boys chased girls who chased boys who chased Mr. G.—who ran. Watching the battle, you could tell **precisely** which guy had a crush on which girl, not to mention who was hiding a secret **contempt** for their band-mate. All **repressed** emotions came out—each balloon bulls-eye a wishful kiss or a **spiteful** slap. It was love and war with water balloons.

With each balloon I threw, I felt my social worries slip away. I could see that band camp wasn't just a **microcosm** of high school, with the same old **posses**. Here, cliques didn't matter. Nor did it matter how short or chubby I was. I nailed Brian, and he nailed me back. I spun around and caught Eleni with another wet one, making her squeal.

But what about Mr. G.? I looked over and caught him sneaking out of the fray. Seeing as I was behind him, I had a perfect shot.

Redundant: adj. excessive, especially using more words than are needed.
Orgy: n. a period of indulgence in a particular activity or emotion, especially something that is disapproved of.
Precise: adj. exactly defined; definite; accurate.
Contempt: n. the act of despising; a feeling of disdain.
Repress: v. to put down; subdue; crush.
Spiteful: adj. full of petty spite; malicious.
Microcosm: n. a miniature copy of something, especially when it represents or stands for a larger whole.
Posse: n. a body of persons; a gang.

I considered the risk for a minute: I was as fresh as a freshman could be. People were still learning my name. Did I dare pelt a *teacher*?

YES! **Impetuously**, I whipped my red balloon straight at Mr. G.

There was a *slap* as the balloon nailed Mr. G. right between the shoulder blades, then a sad little *bloop* as the unexploded water balloon bounced across the grass.

Everyone froze. Mr. G. arched his back in pain. The eyes of one hundred bandies locked on my face, as I grinned **apprehensively**.

Ooops.

Mr. G. turned and picked up my red balloon. Then, with a **diabolical** look in his eye, he yelled the words that changed the next four years of my life: "GET HEANEY!"

The band charged at me, **convulsing** with joy. I turned and fled for my life.

The balloons rained down around me. I dropped to the ground with a silly grin on my face, with Mr. G.'s rallying cry still in my ears. I was no longer **nameless**. I was "HEANEY!", the **rebellious** freshman. Even as they pelted me, my fellow bandies were cheering me. I had been bold. I had **bombarded** authority. And now, I had a place in the band. Sure, it had nothing to do with musical **aptitude**, but it was even better.

Impetuous: adj. sudden and vehement in action; impulsive.

Apprehensive: adj. uneasy or fearful about future events.

Diabolical: adj. connected with the devil or devil worship, or extremely cruel or evil.

Convulse: v. to jerk or shake violently and uncontrollably, sometimes with laughter or a strong emotion.

Nameless: adj. obscure; anonymous.

Rebellious: adj. defiant; resisting control.

Bombard: v. to assail violently; to attack.

Aptitude: n. ability; innate talent for something.

I was in charge of **instigating** fun. I was the Water-**Buffoon**-in-Chief.

❉

When senior year rolled around, life was looking even better. I had grown almost a foot taller, lost the **atrocious** bowl-shaped haircut, and started wearing Hawaiian shirts day in and day out. Much more than the Grateful Dead getup, the Hawaiian shirts fit my **eccentric** personality: loud, **quirky**, and colorful. They announced that I was anything but a **conformist** and became my trademark. To my own amazement, my new **iconoclastic** image even helped my love life. I dated a member of the color guard—a blonde and **willowy** girl named Katrijn.

More importantly, I became an official leader of the band. The head of the trombone section graduated and passed the **mantle** of leadership down to me, giving me the chance to shape a new generation of bandies. I was nervous at first, and

Instigate: v. to urge or stimulate.

Buffoon: n. someone who amuses others by clowning, by joking, or by ridiculous behavior.

Atrocious: adj. appallingly bad; so ugly in taste or appearance as to revile.

Eccentric: adj. deviating from usual or recognized form; irregular; odd.

Quirk: n. a peculiar trait.

Conformist: n. a person who adopts or accepts the usual standards or practices of a group without questioning them.

Iconoclast: n one who challenges cherished beliefs or traditional institutions.

Willowy: adj. slim, graceful, and elegant, partly because of being tall.

Mantle: n. a role or position, especially one that can be passed from one person to another.

irresponsibly covered for it by making my **influx** of new trombones do **gratuitous** push-ups. Once I mellowed out a bit, though, I got along quite well with my **underlings**. I helped them **assimilate** to the quirky culture of the band, and in return, they made me proud, becoming the band's loudest, funniest, *and* most talented section.

Ed was our blond, gentle giant, always willing to be the **butt** of a stupid joke. Then there was Mike, who could've been my **doppelgänger** if he didn't have a thick Brooklyn accent. Pablo was the heart of the trombones, kind enough to **absolve** me for kicking him in the groin (an accident—I swear!). And Sally, our first female trombone in years, brought the innocent smile that tempered our masculine vibe. When we got carried away **harassing** the flutes, Sally always reminded us to play nice.

As the leader of this **diverse** clan, I knew the **onus** was on me to make their band camp experience as wet and wild as my own had been. In case I had forgotten this task, Tim made sure to remind me. That summer, as I was putting my trombone

---

Irresponsible: adj. not having or showing any care for the consequences of personal actions.
Influx: n. a sudden arrival of a large number of people or things.
Gratuitous: adj. freely given; unnecessary; being without cause.
Underling: n. one who is in a subordinate or inferior position.
Assimilate: v. to take in and incorporate; to absorb.
Butt: n. someone or something that is an object of ridicule or contempt for other people.
Doppelgänger: n. someone who looks very like another person.
Absolve: v. to pardon; free from penalty.
Harass: v. to annoy by repeated attacks.
Diverse: adj. essentially different; varied.
Onus: n. a burden; a charge.

away after a hot rehearsal, he **sauntered** up and lifted his cool-guy sunglasses.

"Yo, Chris, we gotta make this the best water-balloon fight the band has *ever* seen," he said in his most sincere, **artless** voice, closing his eyes when he said "ever" and pinching his thumbs and forefingers together, like he had just smelled a **sumptuous** feast.

Ah, Tim. Some people change in high school. Others do not.

"And we gotta soak Mr. G.! One! Last! Time!" he added. Tim was not the most **eloquent** guy.

But he had a point. In the last couple years, the water-balloon war at band camp had been **lackluster**. Mr. G. had tried everything to **suppress** our ritual. He no longer even **deigned** to take part in it. Without an authority figure to target, the game had lost some of its thrill. It was up to the band leaders to **salvage** the tradition.

To my **chagrin**, Tim was also a bandleader. In fact, he was the drum major, the official student head of the band. He had not only grown **complacent** with his power, but he seemed to assume that he could hit on any girl in the band.

And now here Tim was inviting me to **conspire** with him.

Saunter: v. to walk at an easy unhurried pace.
Artless: adj. without guile or deception.
Sumptuous: adj. lavish; luxurious; grand.
Eloquent: adj. having the power to speak vividly and appropriately; persuasive or expressive.
Lackluster: adj. lacking energy, excitement, enthusiasm, or passion.
Suppress: v. to restrain; abolish.
Deign: v. to do something in a way that shows it is a great favor and almost beneath dignity to do it; to stoop.
Salvage: v. to save.
Chagrin: n. mental disquiet or grief; self-dissatisfaction.
Complacent: adj. self-satisfied.
Conspire: v. to agree together especially to do something wrong or illegal; plot secretly.

Thankfully, I was a step ahead of him. I was creating my own **innovative** battle plan—full of fat balloons and bitter **treason**. And the person I planned to betray was not Mr. G. This year, my dear friend Tim was the target.

To sweeten my **vindictive** plot, I was hoping to make Mr. G. my partner in crime. Over the last three years he and I had developed an odd sort of friendship. Freshman year I became **notorious** for correcting his loose use of the word "**seraphim**." But instead of scowling at my **pedantic** comment, Mr. G. made a joke of it and handed me a dollar in front of the band. From that moment on, I was the only band member who could trade **quips** with him like an old friend.

Though we had grown close, I still wasn't sure Mr. G. would buy into my water-balloon scheme. On the way to Camp Bernie, I approached the front of the bus to find him. Mr. G. was sitting alone, intently studying a clipboard of field positions. I sat down and began my **supplication**.

"Mr. G., I wanted to talk to you about the water-balloon fight."

"Not going to do it, Chris," Mr. G. responded in a **terse**

Innovative: adj. introducing something new; novel.
Treason: n. betrayal of trust.
Vindictive: adj. disposed to seek revenge; bitter.
Notorious: adj. well-known for some undesirable feature or act.
Seraphim: n. an angel of the highest rank in the traditional medieval hierarchy of nine categories of angels.
Pedantic: adj. relating to one who makes a show of knowledge.
Quip: n. a witty remark, especially one made on the spur of the moment.
Supplication: n. a humble appeal to someone who has the power to grant a request.
Terse: adj. saying much in few words.

voice. He gave me a **sidelong** glance from his clipboard. "I'm tired of being the target. Aren't you?"

I **grimaced**. He had a **valid** point. The band tradition had become:

1. Soak Mr. G.!
2. Soak Heaney!
3. Repeat!

"I *gueeeess*," I conceded for a moment, before moving on to the meat of my scheme. "And that's exactly why Tim can't wait to get you"—I **mimicked** Tim's tough-guy Jersey accent—"*one, last, time!*"

Mr. G. laughed at my **mocking impersonation** of our cocky bandleader. I hoped this meant Mr. G.'s **skepticism** was fading. If nothing else, I had **piqued** his interest.

"So that's why we're going to turn the tables," I went on. "In the middle of the war, Tim will give a signal for the band to soak you. But what if the band turns around and soaks *him* instead?"

It was a betrayal of **epic** proportions. Mr. G.'s eyes were hidden behind square sunglasses, but I could detect an **inkling**

Sidelong: adj. directed to the side or slating to one side.
Grimace: v. to twist the face in a way that expresses disgust or pain.
Valid: adj. well-grounded or justifiable.
Mimic: v. to imitate, especially derisively.
Mock: v. to ridicule; deride.
Impersonation: n. assuming the character of another; imitation of another person's voice, mannerisms, etc.
Skepticism: n. an attitude marked by a tendency to doubt what others accept to be true.
Pique: v. to arouse the interest of.
Epic: adj. extending beyond the usual or ordinary, especially in size or scope.
Inkling: n. a hint.

of a smile on his lips. Tim might be his student leader, but Mr. G. had a **sardonic** sense of humor.

"So when Tim says 'GET HIM,'" Mr. G. slowly repeated the **tentative** plan back, "We all get *Tim* instead?"

"Right," I replied.

"And I stay dry?" Mr. G. asked, **savoring** these **provisions**.

"Dry as a bone. You have my word," I promised. I had no interest in **coercing** Mr. G. into a scheme that would spoil our dynamic.

"You've got a deal." Mr. G. declared. "It's Tim's year to drown."

YES! I jumped to my feet.

"But Chris?" Mr. G. added. "If I get even *one* water balloon thrown at me, I'll have your head." I saluted and turned on my heel, smiling at Mr. G. We had a **pact**.

When the bus finally delivered us to Camp Bernie, I spent the next three days psyching up Tim for the fake plan to nail Mr. G. Meanwhile, I **disseminated** the *real* plan (to nail *Tim* instead) to the rest of the band. **Duplicity** was a new thing for me, and I sort of liked it.

Tim also played the **braggart**, prattling on about how his **tactics** would take down Mr. G.

Sardonic: adj. sneering; sarcastic; cynical.
Tentative: adj. not fully worked out or developed.
Savor: v. to enjoy something with unhurried appreciation.
Provision: n. a measure taken beforehand to deal with a need or contingency.
Coerce: v. to compel by force.
Pact: n. an agreement.
Disseminate: v. to disperse throughout; scatter.
Duplicity: n. bad faith; dissimulation; hypocrisy; double dealing.
Braggart: n. a boastful person.
Tactics: n. maneuvers especially in a battle.

At first, I thought Tim's loudmouthing was **innocuous**. He was just making a bit of a fool of himself, right? But I soon grew paranoid that his bragging would **jeopardize** the plan. If a member of Mr. G.'s staff overheard one of Tim's **declamations**, he might think that we were actually planning to strike against Mr. G. What if he told Mr. G. this and **discredited** me? With the water-balloon war just hours away, Mr. G. might **speculate** that I was playing a **merciless** joke on him. There would be no time to **refute** the misunderstanding.

This very worry was ballooning in my mind when I heard screams rip out of the freshman-girls' cabin.

I dropped my pile of water grenades and ran to find a **gaggle** of five **frantic** flute players.

"MISTER GEEE!" they screamed.

Between squeals and gasps, the story spilled out. The girls had been prepping for battle when Mr. G. and Rick—Mr. G.'s trumpet director, whom I had seen listening to Tim boast—made a surprise attack and **confiscated** their balloons, running off with the **loot**.

Innocuous: adj. harmless.
Jeopardize: v. to put someone or something at risk of being harmed or lost.
Declamation: n. a speech of presentation spoken in a formal and theatrical style.
Discredit: v. to injure the reputation of; destroy confidence in.
Speculate: v. to meditate or ponder; reflect.
Merciless: adj. pitiless; cruel; without mercy.
Refute: v. to defeat by argument or proof; disprove.
Gaggle: n. a flock of geese, or a group of people, especially a noisy or disorderly group.
Frantic: adj. frenzied; wild with excitement, pain, or fear.
Confiscate: v. to take someone's property with authority, or appropriate it for personal use as if with authority.
Loot: n. booty seized in war; plunder; spoils; something stolen.

This didn't sound good. I looked over the shoulders of the frantic flutists and saw Mr. G. and Rick running off through the trees. Both were carrying a mesh bag with enough balloons to **submerge** a Hummer.

"YOU'RE DEAD, HEANEY!" yelled Mr. G., **sequestering** himself in the staff cabin.

I smacked myself on the forehead. Mr. G. had assumed the worst. It was too late to **exonerate** myself.

Tim ran up behind me. "What's up?" he asked.

"Mr. G. knows the plan. We've **bungled** everything." I took a breath, quickly **fabricating** a bogus plan. I wasn't going to let this glitch **thwart** my effort. I looked back at Tim. "We're just going to have to strike the staff cabin. And you'll have to lead us."

Tim opened his mouth to reply, but I cut him off **dismissively**. "Just get your balloons and meet us at the field! **Hustle**!"

It felt good to give the kid orders.

I ran toward the field. This was a **dilemma** I hadn't planned for. I would have to **improvise** a way to soak Tim five minutes before all hell broke loose.

Submerge: v. to place or plunge underwater.
Sequester: v. to put someone in an isolated or lonely place.
Exonerate: v. to relieve of blame or accusation; exculpate; clear.
Bungle: to cause something to fail through carelessness or incompetence.
Fabricate: v. to concoct falsely; to invent.
Thwart: v. to prevent from accomplishing a purpose; frustrate; baffle.
Dismiss: v. to reject serious consideration of.
Hustle: v. to go somewhere or do something fast or hurriedly.
Dilemma: n. a problem involving a difficult choice.
Improvise: v. to act or compose something, especially a sketch, play, song, or piece of music, without any preparation or set text to follow.

There was a **corps** of about seventy-five bandies waiting on the field, water balloons in hand. I sent my trombones Pablo and Mike to act as lookouts, giving them strict orders to cry like dying llamas when Tim came our way. They ran off, and I pushed into the center of the circle.

"Change of plans," I panted, then launched into an **extemporaneous** speech. "Mr. G. chickened out. We're still going to soak Tim, but this is how it's going to work—" I looked up and was startled to see a few blank faces. Had no one been paying attention? I went on, hoping the **conviction** in my voice would win them over. "Tim's going to give some silly speech about how we're attacking the staff cabin. But when I yell, 'NOW!'" I paused, trying to lay emphasis on the most **crucial** piece of the plot, "We let loose with the balloons and SOAK TIM!"

There was a sound like a dying llama. Pablo and Mike had **espied** the enemy.

"OK?" I asked.

"YEAH!" My loyal trombones shouted the loudest. Bless them.

I looked to my fellow seniors, who had seen me rise the band totem pole, from nerdy novice to water-balloon grandmaster. They gave me a **deferential** nod, smiling. Perhaps my **insurgence** wasn't so half-baked after all.

Corps: n. a military force that carries out specialized duties, or a group of people who work together or are associated.

Extemporaneous: adj. made, spoken or performed without previous preparation; improvised at the moment.

Conviction: n. firmness of belief or opinion, or a belief of opinion that is held firmly.

Crucial: adj. decisive; critical.

Espy: v. to catch site of.

Deferential: adj. respectful.

Insurgence: n. a rebellion or uprising against a government.

Tim ran into the circle, looking **swarthy** in swim trunks and a white singlet. "Listen up guys!" he began, taking a knee in the center like a football coach. "Change of plans!"

I stood behind Tim, my arms crossed, and glared at the back of his head. I could feel my fellow bandies send me **anxious** glances. But I kept my eyes on the enemy with a stone face, hoping my **gravity** would set an example.

Meanwhile, Tim was clueless. He went on with his **exposition**, "Mr. G. and the staff are in their cabin, and they got about thirty balloons. Now we got them way outgunned." He flexed his right bicep. "So I figger we just gotta run right at 'em. We're gonna get a little wet, but—"

It was too good to be true.

I had perfect aim, and all of the backup I could possibly want.

This was the moment I had been waiting four years for.

"NOW!!" I commanded the band, firing the red balloon in my right hand, quickly following it with the yellow balloon in my left. Both nailed Tim right in the back, bursting against his singlet and soaking him. He looked **incredulous**, like he didn't believe I'd just made him the **protomartyr** of the water-balloon war.

I grinned like a **maniac**. But as my eyes refocused, I saw that my seventy-five bandies were glaring at me like I had two heads.

Swarthy: adj. with a dark and often weather-beaten complexion.
Anxious: adj. full of anxiety; worried.
Gravity: adj. serious behavior; solemnity.
Exposition: n. speech or writing intended to explain or convey information.
Incredulous: adj. unwilling to admit or accept what is offered as true; expressing disbelief.
Protomartyr: n. the first martyr in a cause or region.
Maniac: n. a person raving with madness.

I was the only one who had thrown a balloon. No one had followed my command.

Instantly, I panicked, assuming *I* was the true victim of all the double-crossing. But it wasn't **treachery** on their faces, it was **hesitation**. In other words, as a college application might want it phrased: "poor leadership."

But I wasn't about to give up.

"NOW!!" I boomed in a **resolute** voice. The bandies remained **static**, not moving an inch.

Tim recovered from the shock of water grenades and gave me a glare that almost **singed** my eyebrows.

Here we go again, I thought to myself. The only thing left to do now was what I did as a freshman: Run like hell.

I took off down a hill, **shrieking** at my bandies, "GET TIM! GET TIM!"

Tim ran after me and the bandies finally snapped out of their **ambivalent** daze. They chased after us like sharks smelling blood.

Tim was a speedy guy, and I had a lot less **dexterity** as a sprinter. He soon tackled me from behind and we hit the dirt. When the band caught up, Tim used me as a shield for the **onslaught** of balloons he knew was **inevitable**. Water cruise missiles exploded on my exposed chest and legs, blowing up

---

Treachery: n. violation of allegiance or faith; betrayal of trust.
Hesitation: n. a falter or pause.
Resolute: adj. steadfast; firm and unwavering.
Static: adj. fixed; stationary; stagnant.
Singe: v. to burn slightly or superficially.
Shriek: n. a sharp, shrill outcry or scream, caused by agony or terror.
Ambivalence: n. mixed or conflicting feelings.
Dexterity: n. ease and skill in physical movement.
Onslaught: n. a violent attack.
Inevitable: adj. unavoidable.

mud and latex **shrapnel** around us. No one cared any longer *who* they **demolished**. It was war.

"MISTER GEE!" Someone in the mob recalled our favorite victim and yelled out his name. Everyone began running toward the staff cabin, leaving Tim and me laying in the mud, **inert**. I expected the worst.

As Tim unpinned me and got up, I lay on my back. The sun **blazed** overhead, but Tim's head blocked it out, casting his face in shadows. He raised his hand and I flinched, certain he was going to conclude all of this nonsense with a punch to the nose.

But Tim was just readjusting his sunglasses. The punch had been **illusory**. If he wasn't going to throw a punch, would Tim give me a bitter **invective**?

"Tim, I—" I quickly searched for something to **reconcile** us.

He grabbed my arm and hauled me out of the mud.

"It's OK, man," he offered, cocking his head. "You got it worse than me."

I looked down and saw my shirt was soaked through. True.

Tim smiled, offering me quick **absolution**, "But we still got work to do."

Shrapnel: n. metal balls or fragment that are scattered when a shell bomb or bullet explodes.

Demolish: v. to destroy a building or other structure completely, or to beat an opponent very convincingly, especially in sports or debate.

Inert: adj. having no power to move or act.

Blaze: v. to burn brightly; shine.

Illusory: adj. based on or producing an illusion; deceptive.

Invective: n. an abusive speech; vituperation.

Reconcile: v. to restore to union and friendship; to settle differences.

Absolution: n. forgiveness of sins; remission of punishment for sins.

Off in the distance, our troops were laying **siege** upon the staff cabin. They needed our backup. Nearly all the balloons had been **exhausted**. Tim and I ran off to join them. One musician after another was throwing himself at the **bulwarks** of the cabin porch. I watched a **valorous** saxophonist named Joe make it up two steps before being bowled over by a blue balloon. Then, Rick, the trumpet coach, darted out and stole Joe's balloons. Without them, I didn't see how our attack could **sustain** itself.

That's when I **discerned** a head of curly reddish-blond hair among the staff members in the cabin. It popped out of a window, then quickly disappeared. Mr. G.: the very reason I had joined marching band four years ago. The time for **diplomacy** was over. My plan finally felt **definitive**. I knew exactly what I needed to do.

Tim handed me a purple balloon. "Go for it, man," he said, running to rescue some of the squealing flutists.

I broke into a sprint—no easy task in the muddy remains of a water-balloon massacre—and shouted as I picked up speed. My trombones, darting in and out of the crossfire, cheered and **reunited** behind me in a flying V as I leapt up the steps of the

Siege: n. a prolonged effort to gain or overcome something.
Exhaust: v. to use up all that is available of something.
Bulwark: n. a wall-like structure to keep out attackers.
Valorous: adj. valiant; possessing courage or acting with bravery.
Sustain: v. to maintain; support; keep alive.
Discern: v. to distinguish by the eye or intellect; perceive; discriminate.
Diplomacy: n. tact or skill in conducting any kind of negotiations; handling affairs without arousing hostility.
Definitive: adj. conclusive; fixed; final.
Reunite: v. to bring people together, or come together, after a separation.

porch. I **brandished** a fat purple water balloon and cocked my throwing arm back just as Mr. G. stepped out from the cover of a bunk bed, framing himself in the doorway.

"HEANEY!" He shouted my name.

"MISTER GEE!" I yelled back.

At that, we both let our balloons fly.

Time slowed to a **glacial** pace.

Mr. G. ducked at the last second and my purple bullet exploded on the **adjacent** bunk. His yellow grenade, however, punched me in the left shoulder.

I hollered at my trombone troops for reinforcements. "Throw me another balloooooon!"

Gentle Ed **complied**, tossing me a red one. I caught it in midair and I spun back to the cabin.

However, before I could launch the last water grenade of my high school career, a black nozzle shoved itself in my face. This was not a water balloon. It was not any weapon with water in it. This was a fire extinguisher, ready to blast my **fatuous** grin all the way to Wisconsin.

Rick stood behind the nozzle, his mouth twisted into a **sneer**.

Poof!

He fired straight at me. Camp Bernie disappeared in a

Brandish: v. to wave (as a weapon) threateningly; to exhibit in an aggressive way.

Glacial: adj. moving or advancing extremely slowly.

Adjacent: adj. near or close, especially adjoining.

Comply: v. to obey or conform to something, for example, a rule, law, wish or regulation.

Fatuous: adj. silly; foolish, especially in an unconscious manner.

Sneer: n. a facial expression of scorn or hostility in which the upper lip may be raised.

gossamer cloud of white foam and smoke. My mouth filled with **putrid** chemicals.

I tried to pull back, but my feet couldn't get any **traction** on the wet steps. A second blast caught me in the chest, frosting my Hawaiian shirt like a blizzard and sending me flying. I **collapsed** in the mud, wiping the foam from my eyes.

Next, I opened my eyes to a blue sky. Ed, his blond hair **luminous** in the sun, pulled me up from the mud.

"It's over, Ed," I said **dejectedly**. "We should **concede** defeat."

"Why?" Ed replied. "That was awesome." Ed looked genuinely appreciative for the disaster plan I had led the band on.

"After you got hit with the fire extinguisher," he recounted, excitedly, "Mike grabbed a bucket and **doused** Rick for you. Oh! And this is the best part: Pablo found a hose."

"Really? A hose?" I replied. If there was one weapon that was better than a fire extinguisher, it was a garden hose.

I looked over at the cabin. Sure enough, Rick had been totally soaked.

Gossamer: adj. light, delicate, or insubstantial.

Putrid: adj. rotten; foul.

Traction: n. the adhesive friction between a moving object and the surface on which it is moving.

Collapse: v. to fall down suddenly, generally as a result of damage, structural weakness, or lack of support.

Luminous: adj. giving out light.

Dejected: adj. sad; depressed.

Concede: v. to admit or acknowledge something, often grudgingly or with reluctance; to surrender.

Douse: v. to plunge or submerge someone or something in water, or to put a lot of water or other liquid on someone or something.

Meanwhile, Pablo **hustled** along the porch with a long green hose, unseen by the rest of the staffers.

Yes! I thought, now proud of my suicide mission.

"Want another balloon, Chris?" Ed offered.

I saw Mr. G.'s red head pop back up in the cabin window. As soon as he lay eyes on Pablo and Pablo's hose, Mr. G.'s head ducked back down. For a moment, I felt like I was back in eighth grade—an overweight kid fantasizing about **chaos** and new chances. High school hadn't turned out exactly as I had dreamed—few chem-lab explosions and even fewer hot cheerleaders. But in many ways—the ways that mattered—the past four years had been even better than I could have foreseen. You might say I was finally at the top of my game.

Now, it was time to take on a **noncombatant** role.

"No thanks." I smiled at Ed and shook my head. "I'm gonna dry off, buddy. You're in charge now." I started to walk away. "Oh, and Ed?" I paused, grinning widely.

"Yeah, Chris?"

"Tell Pablo to point the hose in the right window. Someone in there's waiting for a shower."

Hustle: v. to go somewhere or do something fast or hurriedly.
Chaos: n. the absence of form or order; utter confusion.
Noncombatant: adj. not engaged in combat.

❋ **Chris Heaney** grew up in northern New Jersey. He brought his trombone with him when he went to Yale, but it started gathering dust in his closet. The trombone is still mad at him. Chris majored in Latin American studies and is now a writer, currently in Peru on a Fulbright Fellowship. Fun fact: On Sundays in February in Peru, kids get to nail adults with water balloons and shaving cream. It almost makes him nostalgic for band camp. Almost.

3

CONFESSIONS OF A ROAD HAZARD

Colleen Kinder

When my dad taught me to drive, he assumed he was my only teacher. What he didn't know was that since I was fifteen, my big sister Katie had been taking me to the **vacant** parking lot of a community college and lending me the driver's seat. What *Katie* didn't know was that I had **cajoled** my *other* big sister, Molly, into letting me practice on back roads of our quiet suburb, while she watched **vigilantly** from shotgun.

"Don't tell Dad," both sisters **threatened**.

"Or Katie," Molly added.

"Molly either," warned Katie.

My sisters, like my father, believed that they were **ushering** me through the great teenage rite of passage: earning the driver's license. Meanwhile, I was **dissembling** to my whole family in order to speed through the **didactic** phase as quickly as

Vacant: adj. having no contents; empty; devoid of something.
Cajole: v. to persuade by flattery, especially in the face of reluctance; gentle urging.
Vigilantly: adj. alert to detect danger.
Threaten: v. to utter threats (against).
Usher: v. to contribute to the beginning of; to conduct to a place like an usher.
Dissemble: v. to give a false impression about; conceal one's real motives.
Didactic: adj. instructive; intended to teach.

I could. Newly sixteen, I believed that a driver's license was my ticket to freedom and longed to **procure** it in record time.

My dad had **accompanied** both my sisters to their road tests and he liked to add some **fanfare** to the event. Just like he took pride in teaching us all to ride bikes, having the last hand on our two-speeds before letting us zip off on our own, my dad **cherished** road-test day. Once his daughters passed the **momentous** exam, he would treat them to lunch at Ted's Hot Dogs, a favorite eatery in Buffalo, New York. Hot dogs at Ted's were long, greasy, and heaped with toppings. While a foot-long was the short-term prize for acing the road test, the long-term reward was even sweeter: the Whale.

The Whale was a Buick Roadmaster: a **voluptuous** white mass of a station wagon. It had wood siding and what we called a "bubble"—a **peculiar** sunroof bulging across the midsection of the car's roof. My mom bought the Whale when I was in fifth grade, selecting it not for its dazzling looks, but because it was "a tank." My mother—wise **matriarch** that she is—could already imagine her trio of sweet little girls as teenage drivers and she had one concern: collisions.

We named it the Whale not just for its **enormity**, but because the silver grill of the car smiled like the maw of a humpback. There wasn't a single right angle on the thing, only curves and bulges. The Whale had terrible pickup—as if an anvil was buckled into

Procure: v. to get possession of.
Accompany: v. to go with; be associated with.
Fanfare: n. a flourish of trumpets; ceremony; ostentation.
Cherish: v. to hold dear; treat with affection.
Momentous: adj. of great consequence; important.
Voluptuous: adj. suggesting sensual pleasure by fullness of form.
Peculiar: adj. odd; curious.
Matriarch: n. a woman having chief responsibility in a household.
Enormity: n. the quality or state of being huge.

each of the car's eight seats. But it coasted with the slow grace of a sea monster, **careening** down hills with **menacing velocity**.

By the time I reached driving age, my sisters had already done a fine job breaking in the Whale. The seats were **sullied** with food stains. The trunk window wore bumper stickers that shouted their pride in Ireland, in sports, and in our all-girl's Catholic high school: Holy Angels Academy. Katie and Molly had also made the Whale a familiar sight around North Buffalo—a **mammoth** teenager taxi that carted athletic teams to afternoon practices and returned at night with dressed-up, perfumed **versions** of the same young ladies.

The day my dad took me to my road test, I was **pondering** an **exultant** return to Holy Angels in the Whale. I would waltz back into sixth period, holding my head high. By seventh period, the news would be **disseminated** throughout the school. All fifty of my female classmates were **cognizant** that I was braving the Department of Motor Vehicles exam. I was one of the first in our tiny class to do so, and let's just say I was known for taking tests very, very seriously.

"Hi," I said to my road-test examiner when she opened the car door. I had been expecting a man.

"Hi," she replied in a **frigid** voice. I decided against the

---

Careen: v. to sway from side to side; to lurch.
Menace: v. to pose a threat to.
Velocity: n. quickness or rate of motion; speed.
Sully: v. to stain; defile.
Mammoth: n. gigantic; immense.
Version: n. a particular form or variant of something.
Ponder: v. to reflect (upon, over); consider deeply.
Exultant: adj. rejoicing; filled with great triumph.
Disseminate: v. to disperse throughout; to scatter.
Cognizant: n. knowledgeable of something especially through personal experience.
Frigid: adj. chilly, in manner; formal.

amicable small talk I had prepared. Instead, I pulled out into traffic and made a three-point turn, **violating** the very first rule of road tests. I did not look over my shoulder.

The violations piled up from there, **accruing** every time my examiner scribbled on her pink slip of paper. After the **reckless** three-point turn came the reckless lane change, followed by a reckless detour down a one-way street—the wrong way. The parallel park was the icing on the cake of my **abysmal** road test. My first attempt to back in the car landed us about four feet from the curb. I looked at my road-test examiner and **grimaced**, hoping we could just call it quits right there, in the middle of the road. I was ready to **capitulate**. Yes ma'am, I'm a totally **incompetent** driver.

She must have agreed. At the bottom of my pink sheet, she advised me to "practice more."

My dad drove us to Ted's Hot Dogs anyway. But I stayed inside the car and said I didn't want anything—not even a foot-long could **placate** my shame. I had known today would be a major **milestone**, but hadn't expected the milestone to begin with the glaring letter F.

I returned home and practiced as frequently as my parents would lend me the wheel. During this **interlude** between road

---

Amicable: adj. neighborly; friendly; showing goodwill.
Violate: v. to break, or infringe, as a law or contract.
Accrue: v. to accumulate or be added periodically.
Reckless: adj. daring; imprudent; foolhardy.
Abysmal: adj. immeasurably low or wretched.
Grimace: v. to twist the face, expressive of pain, disgust.
Capitulate: v. to surrender; to give up.
Incompetent: adj. not fit or capable.
Placate: v. to pacify; soothe.
Milestone: n. an important event in life.
Interlude: n. intervening time, period, or stage.

tests, my dad and I took a more **measured** approach to drivers' education. We parallel parked all over our suburb. We had three-point-turn marathons. He made me check, recheck, and triple-check the mirrors like my **narcissism** depended on it.

The second time my Dad and I pulled up to the road-test site, he was **optimistic**.

"*Now* you're going to nail this," he **reiterated**, like a **mantra**.

As soon as I began my road test, I knew my dad was right. I *was* more prepared. I pulled into traffic **cautiously**; I **navigated** one-way streets in that one way that they were supposed to be driven; I even slid the car into a **comely** parallel park. Everything about the test drive felt **auspicious**. When we neared a red light and my tester told me to turn back toward our starting point, my pulse grew rapid. *Woo-hoo!* But this quickened pulse must have pumped **superfluous** blood to my pedal foot, because I cruised straight through the light. Yes, the red one.

My stomach instantly grew heavy. My examiner was writing something. I did not want to see that something, nor my father. Minutes later, when my dad read the pink slip of paper, I tried to explain that it wasn't as **flagrant** a violation as it seemed. I hadn't so much *run* the red light as I had *glided* through it. But my

---

Measured: adj. regulated by measure; deliberate; calculated.
Narcissism: n. excessive concern for oneself.
Optimistic: adj. the belief that good will prevail.
Reiterate: v. to repeat; say or do again.
Mantra: n. a word or motto that embodies a principle; a repeated word or statement.
Cautiously: adv. warily; acting with fear.
Navigate: v. to sail or steer.
Comely: adj. good-looking.
Auspicious: adj. well omened; suggesting success.
Superfluous: adj. more than is needed.
Flagrant: adj. outrageous; offensive.

defense was **futile**. My dad didn't believe that my error was **incidental**. On the contrary, he considered it the most **inane** error ever made in the history of repeat road tests. When we drove past Ted's Hot Dogs in silence, I knew my Mom would be **accompanying** me to road test number three.

＊

The Department of Motor Vehicles was **prudent** to keep me off the road as long as they did. When I finally did get my license and the Whale was **bequeathed** to me, I hit the streets of Buffalo with a **vengeance**. Whenever dents or other **flaws** appeared on the car, I blamed one of my sisters. "It must have been Katie." Molly wasn't as easy to make **culpable**, so once Katie was in college, I began to **employ** this handy **rhetorical** defense: "Mom, if I hit something *that* hard, don't you think I would have heard it?"

The **euphoria** of driving alone was everything I expected it to be. Sure, some of the **novelty** wore off when the Buffalo snowstorms turned my morning commute into a **harrowing**

Futile: adj. ineffectual; serving no useful purpose.
Incidental: adj. casual; minor.
Inane: adj. void of sense or intelligence; silly.
Accompany: v. to go with; be associated with.
Prudent: adj. judicious; wise.
Bequeath: v. to hand down; give or leave by will.
Vengeance: n. retributive punishment; revenge.
Flaw: n. defect; imperfection.
Culpable: adj. deserving censure; blameworthy.
Employ: v. to use; give occupation to.
Rhetorical: adj. asked merely for effect, with no answer expected.
Euphoria: n. a feeling of well-being or elation.
Novelty: n. the quality of being new or fresh; a new experience or thing.
Harrowing: adj. distressing; extremely disturbing.

video game, but I **relished** the freedom nonetheless. The Whale became the **linchpin** of my social life. Following the **precedent** my sisters had set, I packed an **inordinate** number of friends into its cabin and got everyone in a **frolicsome** mood.

There's a line in "Love Shack" that my friends and I decided was a **rhapsody** for "our" **shabby** Buick Roadmaster. When the song came on during a Whale joyride, we shouted out with rising **elation**: "I got me a car, it's as big as a whale and it's ABOUT, to SET, SAIL!" Who could **resist** hitting the gas pedal on such a high note? Amazingly, I collected only one speeding ticket in my entire Whale career.

I carted around freshman cross-country runners and crew-team rowers, offering shotgun to whoever sat in it first. Before my track meets, when I was too nervous to **jabber** with anyone, I would jog back to the parking lot and **quarantine** myself in the Whale. This quiet tank was made for meditation. I guess you could call it the world's largest **talisman**. I would lean my head against the Whale's wheel and **visualize** my rivals—from Sacred Heart and Mount Saint Mercy—then imagine **sprinting** by toward the finish line. During high

---

Relish: v. to be pleased with; appreciate.

Linchpin: n. one that serves to hold together parts or elements.

Precedent: n. a person or thing that serves as a model.

Inordinate: adj. beyond proper limits; excessive.

Frolicsome: adj. merrymaking; fun.

Rhapsody: n. an expression of extravagant enthusiasm; a musical composition of irregular form.

Shabby: adj. much worn; run-down.

Elation: n. great joy.

Resist: v. to withstand; oppose.

Jabber: v. to talk rapidly in an incoherent way; chatter.

Quarantine: n. a period of enforced seclusion.

Talisman: n. an object held to act as a charm to bring good fortune.

Visualize: v. to form a mental image of.

Sprint: v. to run at full speed.

school, whether inside or outside of the Whale, I was always racing.

Not only did the car **abet** my extracurricular pursuits, but it affected my **scholarly** work as well. Take psychology class. Our teacher assigned us to "break a social norm" in small groups. It didn't take my classmates and me long to **conspire** a way we could **violate** one of society's rules—on wheels.

"Let's tie Sidney to the top of the Whale," Katie Wopperer (also known as Wopps) declared.

"What social norm would that break?"

"I don't know." Wopps paused. "Riding *inside* the car?"

"As opposed to . . ."

"Riding *outside* the car. Strapped to the roof—like a dead deer."

"Sweet. Do you think Professor Gray will buy that?"

"I dunno. Let's **embellish** it a little—to be safe. We'll tie Sidney to the top of the Whale, and—"

"—Put deer antlers on her!"

"—and go through the McDonald's drive-thru!"

"—and have *her* order the food . . ."

"—a Big Mac . . ."

"—from the *roof*!"

Now *this* was getting good. I still wasn't positive our **ploy** met the assignment requirements, but it sounded **outlandish** enough to **transgress** all sorts of "norms." If nothing else, it

---

Abet: v. to encourage; aid by approval, especially in bad conduct.
Scholarly: adj. related to schools, scholars, or education.
Conspire: v. to agree together especially to do something wrong or illegal; plot secretly.
Violate: v. to break or infringe, as a law or contract.
Embellish: v. to heighten the attractiveness of by adding decorative details.
Ploy: n. a game, an escapade or trick.
Outlandish: adj. unfamiliar; bizarre; odd.
Transgress: v. to break or violate.

would **qualify** as the best homework I'd done in three years of high school.

So we got bungee cords, found deer antlers, and picked up Sidney. She looked at us **quizzically**, as if she was about to **balk**. But **eventually**, Sidney agreed to the plan.

"You rock, Sid. You're going to have a blast up there."

Sid did. We all did. I drove the Whale at an uncharacteristically low speed and turned the corners as **temperately** as someone passing her road test. The only disappointment was how little we **fazed** the McDonald's staff. They passed the Big Mac straight up to our **prostrate** pal and said, "Have a nice day."

Despite the ambition of our McDonald's scheme, we got a B on the assignment. According to our teacher, dressing up your friends as super-size road kill does not directly challenge any **orthodox** behavior in America. The girls who got A's did lame things like stand on the same escalator steps as strangers (Underachievers, if you ask me).

My grades in English class almost suffered as well when I got behind the wheel. While tardy one morning, I followed a slowpoke red pickup truck all the way to school, trailing close enough for our license plates to clink. I didn't realize that the driver of the truck was Mr. Mitchell, the kindly old teacher who wore tweed blazers and began each class period with an

---

Qualify: v. to fill the requirements for a place or occupation; to be fitted for something.

Quizzical: adj. expressive of puzzlement, curiosity, or disbelief.

Balk: v. to stop short and refuse to proceed.

Eventual: adj. happening or to happen finally; ultimate.

Temperate: adj. moderate.

Faze: v. to ruffle; to disturb the composure of; to intimidate.

Prostrate: adj. lying flat; laid low.

Orthodox: adj. approved; conventional.

anecdote about his hometown of five hundred people. That morning, Mr. Mitchell began our third period English class in his **routine** way: with a story.

But instead of transporting us to **quaint** midcentury Troy, Pennsylvania, Mr. Mitchell shared that this morning, some **wanton** road-rager in a white station wagon had stalked him all the way from the suburbs. I didn't bother to raise my hand and own up to the **allegation**. The blush in my cheeks confessed on my behalf.

Outside of Holy Angels, the Whale helped me get into all sorts of trouble. Driving had given me a taste of freedom, and I had an **insatiable** craving for more. My dad noticed that I was on an **autonomy** kick and didn't like it. He decided I had "attitude," and, after a few heated arguments, he **revoked** my driving rights.

Indefinitely.

I was **indignant**. The thought of riding the bus to school was about as **degrading** as singing "Twinkle, Twinkle, Little Star" to the entire Holy Angels student body—naked. The **prospect** of carpooling with other suburbanites left me feeling

---

Anecdote: n. a short narrative of an occurrence; a story.
Routine: adj. customary; habitual; ordinary.
Quaint: adj. pleasingly or strikingly old-fashioned or unfamiliar.
Wanton: adj. unrestrained, wild, reckless.
Allegation: n. an assertion without proof or before proving.
Insatiable: adj. not satisfied.
Autonomy: n. self-governance; independence.
Revoke: v. to repeal; cancel; take away.
Indefinite: adj. having no fixed or specified limit; infinite.
Indignant: adj. feeling or showing anger, especially righteous anger; resentful.
Degrade: v. to demean; to reduce to a lower rank; to lower the dignity of.
Prospect: n. a possibility.

just as **impotent**. So I called Wopps and **groveled** for a ride to school. She **empathized** and gave me a lift. Unlike poor Sidney, I actually got a seat—inside the car.

But I wasn't about to let the Whale **atrophy** in the driveway, nor let my social life **corrode**. Besides, the car's **proximity**—right in front of the house—was too great a temptation. Every time I looked out the window, the Whale grinned at me like a **decoy**. So I waited in bed until my parents were both asleep, **stealthily** grabbed the spare key, revved up the engine as gently as I could, and **stole** away.

Had I lived in California—or any U.S. city less snowy than Buffalo, for that matter—I might have had hope of **exculpating** myself from the crime. But the problem with driving in the North Pole of America is that snow **incriminates** you. Rip out of the driveway at 2 A.M. and two thick lines of evidence will remain when your early-bird father wakes at dawn. My dad soon caught on and took my punishment to a more **drastic** level. Clearly, it wasn't enough to **prohibit** me from driving. The car had to be **confiscated**—completely. He drove the Whale to

Impotent: adj. lacking strength, power, or virility.

Grovel: v. to crawl or be prone upon the earth; to humble oneself.

Empathize: v. to show sympathy for; to identify with or understand another's situation or feelings.

Atrophy: v. to waste away from lack of use or malnutrition.

Corrode: v. to wear out or eat away gradually, especially by chemical action.

Proximity: n. nearness.

Decoy: n. one who allures as into a trap; anything used as a lure.

Stealthy: adj. secret or furtive in action or character.

Steal: v. to go away from; to move secretly or unobserved.

Exculpate: v. to clear from a charge of fault or guilt; exonerate.

Incriminate: v. to show to be involved in a crime; charge; accuse.

Drastic: adj. having extreme and immediate effect; radical; harsh.

Prohibit: v. to forbid; prevent.

Confiscate: v. to take away by authority.

his **remote** warehouse and left it there, out of my reach.

Wopps showed her **fidelity** once again. This time, though, being my **accomplice** required a minor act of **larceny**. One weekend night, she taxied me to the dark parking lot where my car sat, **desolate** as a beached whale and ready to be **liberated**. We deposited the getaway car back at her house and escaped with the Whale, breaking both our curfews and sleeping at the house of a friend whose parents had no idea that the **gargantuan** white Buick in their driveway was Kinder family contraband.

It took me a long time to earn back my dad's **confidence** after playing so many nasty Whale-custody battles with him. For months, as much as I **lobbied** to **recover** my independence, he was **obdurate**. I had proven myself a punk, and there was too much lasting evidence.

By New Year's Eve 1999, though, my dad decided I was finally mature enough to handle the Whale, unchaperoned.

"Tonight's dangerous, Colleen," my dad began, sounding like he'd rehearsed this **exhortation** many times. "There are all sorts of crazy people on the road. I'll let you have the car as long as you promise me you'll behave."

Remote: adj. far away; distant; not closely connected.
Fidelity: n. faithfulness; loyalty.
Accomplice: n. partner in a crime.
Larceny: n. the wrongful taking of another's goods; theft.
Desolate: adj. uninhabited; abandoned.
Liberate: v. to set free.
Gargantuan: adj. enormous; gigantic.
Confidence: n. firm trust, reliance.
Lobby: v. to solicit the support of legislators; to try to influence the actions of.
Recover: v. to get or obtain (something lost) again; regain; save.
Obdurate: adj. resisting entreaty; hard-hearted; stubborn.
Exhortation: n. language intended to incite and encourage.

I nodded, **disingenuously**. When I promised my dad that the Whale would only be driven by a **designated** driver, I didn't specify *who* I would designate. It wasn't so much **perjury** as it was **evasion** of the truth.

I mean, c'mon: It was New Year's. I had offered the Whale Limo Services to my friends but wasn't about to spoil my own fun by playing chauffeur. So I **delegated** the wheel to a friend with the command, "Your turn." She didn't **bemoan** the driving duty much because there was a good chance she wouldn't have to drive at all. We were ringing in the new year at a house party, where every room was open for sleepover guests. So we went ahead and celebrated the new century, while the Whale waited innocently outside.

Like the **denouement** of a bad teenage movie, the hostess's parents came home just after the stroke of twelve. The house party came to a screeching halt, with two **incensed** parents cursing in Greek and chasing us out of their many bedrooms. I ran out into the snow, shoving on my heels, as the partygoers disbanded in all different directions. I jumped into the car of the nearest responsible driver and fled the scene.

The next morning, 11 A.M. on January 1, 2000, the phone rang at the Kinder house.

"Hi, can I speak to Molly?" This was Wopps, **nonchalantly** pretending to be my sister's friend.

Disingenuous: adj. lacking in candor; giving a false appearance.
Designated: adj. one who is appointed.
Perjury: n. the willful giving of false testimony.
Evasion: n. the act of escaping; dodging something.
Delegate: v. to entrust to another; to assign responsibility.
Bemoan: v. to express deep grief or distress over.
Denouement: n. the solution of a plot in a play.
Incense: v. excite to anger or resentment; enrage.
Nonchalantly: adv. coolly; without showing concern; indifferently.

My mom called upstairs for Molly, but did not hang up. Wopps had a **raspy** voice that was unmistakable.

"Do you know where your sister is?" Wopps asked my sister. "We have the Whale, but don't know what to do with it."

Mom heard every word: Daughter = missing, Whale = found. Mom was not happy. Daughter was soon to be dropped off by a teenage boy driving a Volvo.

I didn't even try to **debunk** my mother's suspicions when she told me I was in trouble. I doubted she would appreciate the **extenuating** circumstances of my evening.

There are far better ways to kick off a new millennium than I had. I felt dreadful, and, for the first time in a long time, **penitent**. It's one thing to break rules when you've been **demonized** as the **unruly** teenager. Another thing, however, when your parents finally **accord** you some trust and treat you like a **conscientious** adult. When people believe in you, screwing up really feels like screwing up.

But January 1 is an **opportune** date to change your ways. My **compunction** set me up for a **zealous** New Year's resolution: to behave myself better. To drive more carefully. To start following a rule or two. In the name of the twenty-first century, I would start to mature. Really.

Raspy: adj. harsh; grating.

Debunk: v. to show the falseness of.

Extenuate: v. to lessen the seriousness of; to make light of.

Penitent: adj. repentant; feeling or expressing sorrow.

Demonize: v. to equate a wicked or cruel person; to turn into a demon.

Unruly: adj. not submissive; ungovernable; wild.

Accord: v. to grant or give, especially as due or earned.

Conscientious: adj. careful; guided by conscience; principled.

Opportune: adj. timely; appropriate.

Compunction: n. a slight regret or prick of conscience.

Zealous: adj. devoted; earnest; filled with passion for a person, cause, or ideal.

As for my car, the Whale was more than mature by the year 2000, and barely resembled the Buick my mom had handpicked years earlier. The abuses of its three **hedonistic** drivers were **manifest** all over its exterior and interior. By the time I went off to college, the driver's-side window was jammed shut. The black rubber strips edging the Whale's wooden panels had lost their **adhesion** and sagged off like lame fins. The Whale's tape player would only work with a fork jammed in its mouth, propping up the tape. (This was **appropriate**, since the tape stuck in it was an eighties mix entitled, "Stick a Fork in Me, I'm Done.") Finally, the hood ornament was ripped off and made into a **commemorative** Christmas ornament.

My dad tried to sell the Whale once all three daughters were safely **enlisted** in college. When that didn't work, he attempted **donating** it to Holy Angels. But no one seemed eager to **assume** ownership of our **beloved** road beast. Eventually, the Whale was sent to the junkyard. Though just like I *glided* (not ran) a red light on my road test, I preferred to think of the Whale as "beached" more than "junked." Our car had been **beneficently** put to sleep. It was the end of an era. Or at least the end of many errors.

In hindsight, it's a miracle that I didn't finish off the family car in a **demolition** on the snowy byways of Buffalo, New

Hedonistic: adj. living in pursuit of pleasure or self-gratification.
Manifest: adj. easily perceived; obvious; apparent.
Adhesion: n. steady or firm attachment.
Appropriate: adj. suitable; fitting for a particular purpose.
Commemorative: adj. honoring or preserving the memory of.
Enlist: v. to enter, as a name on a list; enroll.
Donate: v. to make a gift or contribution.
Assume: v. to take upon oneself; undertake.
Beloved: adj. greatly loved; dear.
Beneficent: adj. doing or producing good; performing acts of charity.
Demolition: n. destruction; the instance of demolishing.

York. Maybe Holy Angels girls have guardian angels on their steering wheels. Come to think of it, all teenage drivers should get patron saints along with their permits. I **nominate** the Whale. After all, he's put in his time in car **purgatory**, rusting in the snow and paying for our sins in dents and dangling pipes. **Canonize** the poor beast.

※ **Colleen Kinder** is a native of Buffalo, New York, where the constant snowfall did nothing to help her driving skills. After attending Yale, she lived in Cuba doing a volunteer project in Havana nursing homes. She is the author of *Delaying the Real World: A Twentysomething's Guide to Seeking Adventure*, a book for young people who want to stay out of the office cubicle. Colleen currently lives in Iowa City, where she writes, teaches, and likes to ride shotgun in other people's cars.

Nominate: v. to propose, as a candidate.
Purgatory: n. a place or state of temporary misery or suffering.
Canonize: v. to designate as a saint; glorify.

4

CONFESSIONS OF A SUMMER-CAMP JUNKIE

Chris Rovzar

For me, the best part of high school was escaping it. I was a summer-camp junkie. Camp Winona had been my summer home since I was nine years old and I worked as a counselor there until college. Situated on a peaceful **lough** in Maine, it was one of those boys camps that fell under the general "wilderness" category. This meant that campers at Camp Winona were kept **frenetically** active all summer, but were never sent home in September with any one spectacular talent, like how to **adeptly** dribble a basketball through your legs, or how to make the clarinet sing.

Unlike the **homogenous** groups of campers at fat camp or God camp, we were truly a **motley** bunch, and damn proud of it. Camp Winona was one of the only places you'd find a book nerd from a Connecticut suburb bunking below a football player from downtown Atlanta. The staff **touted** the camp's

Lough: n. a lake.
Frenetic: adj. wildly excited or active.
Adept: adj. expert; skillful.
Homogeneous: adj. of the same or a similar kind.
Motley: adj. composed of diverse elements; varied.
Tout: v. to praise or publicize loudly or extravagantly; to describe boastfully.

diversity as much as they bragged about its wacky traditions. We had everything, including tribal teams, totems, and, of course, our very own Winona song.

Campers at Winona **idolized** their camp counselors. Teen-age camp counselors are infinitely better than your parents, with whom you have to live (against your will) for the colder portion of the year. They are also younger, funnier, and they know all the hippest slang. Campers at Winona called the camp counselors "Uncle" or, in the case of the few female swimming counselors, "Aunt." This team of aunties and uncles **personified** cool.

Well, that's what I thought, at least. When my turn came to play "Uncle Chris," this **illusion** was quickly **debunked**. Camp Winona gave counselors the **prerogative** of what age group to work with. As far as I was concerned, it was a no-brainer. I could **attest** to the fact that the older campers were terrors (after all, I had been one of them). Whoever's idea it was to **corral** as many thirteen-year-old boys as possible and put them all in a square room with no video games has obviously never been to Camp Winona.

Because adolescence was **wretched** enough the first time around, I opted for the "junior" group of campers aged seven to eleven. It didn't take much to impress the juniors. Come to

Diversity: n. variety; the state of being different.
Idolize: v. to love or admire to excess; to worship as a god.
Personify: v. to be the embodiment of; to represent as a person.
Illusion: n. a misleading image; something that deceives or misleads intellectually.
Debunk: v. to show the falseness of; to expose as exaggerated.
Prerogative: n. a special right, power, or privilege.
Attest: v. to affirm to be true or genuine; to authenticate officially.
Corral: v. to pen up; enclose.
Wretched: adj. miserable; very unfortunate.

think of it, soap on a rope was enough of a **novelty** to keep them **riveted** all summer long. The director assigned me to Tent Three. The term "tent" was meant more as a **domain** than an actual physical shelter. You see, the "tent" was actually half of a log cabin, divided by plywood walls riddled with peepholes and **ribald** grafitti. While the older kids were **banished** to actual military-style platform tents, the young ones were afforded the **extravagance** of walls and a solitary light bulb, to which the moths had a strong **affinity**.

Along with Tent Three came four children: a **wily** Dominican boy named Gonzalo, a slightly **effeminate** redhead from Boston named Johnny, a **maniacal** genius named Stevie from Greenwich, and a quiet, shy Chinese boy named Spencer, who had been adopted by a Maryland family.

Conveniently for my social life (not to mention my sanity), all my best friends were counselors in Junior. We were a ragtag crew, but we did our best to make sure the boys remained alive. The other counselor who lived in my cabin was named Karl, and he was in charge of Tent Four. He was incredibly athletic, **interminably** patient, and always **amicable**. Coincidentally,

Novelty: n. something new or unusual.
Riveted: v. attracted or completely attentive.
Domain: n. a region marked by some physical feature.
Ribald: adj. coarsely humorous; using indecent humor.
Banish: v. to drive out or remove from a home or place.
Extravagance: n. an instance of excess; an excessive outlay of money.
Affinity: n. an attraction to or liking for something.
Wily: adj. crafty; sly.
Effeminate: adj. marked by excessive delicacy; having traits traditionally considered feminine.
Maniacal: adj. frenzied; excessively excited.
Interminable: adj. having or seeming to have no end.
Amicable: adj. friendly; neighborly; showing goodwill.

the two of us had lived together in the same cabin when we were nine-year-old boys.

Karl's kids, of course, **comported** themselves much better than mine. They loved nothing more than to brush their teeth and get into bed at night. On the contrary, Gonzalo, Johnny, Stevie, and Spencer were only **satiated** when I drove to Portland at midnight the day the third Harry Potter book came out. It was this night, while **careening** down pitch-black Maine roads, that I realized it takes a hell of a lot more than **aloofness** to be "cool" in the eyes of a little boy.

✳

On the first morning of the summer season, I was awoken at 6 A.M. by a muffled **whimper**. At first, I assumed it was the director's old drunk dog that sometimes **perambulated** before dawn. But when I sat up, I saw Spencer, the eight-year-old Asian boy, sitting up in bed. His face was wet with tears.

"What's up, Spencer? Why you up so early?" I asked **drowsily**, shuffling across the wooden floor to his bed.

"I miss my mom," he said.

"I understand, buddy. Want to go for a walk?"

"OK."

He pulled on a pair of "campies," the gray-and-maroon

Comport: v. to behave (oneself).
Satiate: v. to satisfy fully.
Careen: v. to sway from side to side; to lurch.
Aloof: adj. distant; removed; indifferent.
Whimper: v. to make a low whining sound.
Perambulate: v. to walk about.
Drowsily: adv. sleepily.

camp uniform, and we walked outside of the tent. Our strategy was to keep them active, because kids tend to grow more homesick when they're **indolent**. Besides, I had to consider the domino effect. One crying kid can become five crying kids faster than you can say "We sent Fido to live on a big farm."

"So you're feeling a little homesick?" I asked, squatting down to the ground. "Here, hop on my back."

"Yeah," Spencer said. He got up on a rock and **clambered** onto my back.

I began walking him down the line of tents, across the **gnarled** roots and orange pine needles that carpeted the ground.

"I know it's nice to be around your parents. I like my house better than I like our cabin. Cabin doesn't smell like home at first. And nobody helps you make your bed."

"You could help us make our beds," Spencer said.

"Fat chance," I chuckled at his attempt to **bamboozle** me.

"What was your favorite part of camp last year?" I asked him.

"I guess I liked Evening Program." Evening Program was a unit-wide game everyone played after dinner, like capture-the-flag or dodgeball, to tire the kids out before bedtime. Evening Program lowered the **likelihood** of evening rowdiness. We liked to get the **boisterous** energy out of their systems.

"Which Evening Program is your favorite?"

Indolent: adj. lazy; sluggish.
Clamber: v. to climb awkwardly.
Gnarled: adj. full of knots; twisted into a state of deformity.
Bamboozle: v. to deceive by underhanded methods.
Likelihood: n. probability; expectancy.
Boisterous: adj. noisy and violent; rowdy.

"I like Greased Watermelon."

"You like the water games? I hear you're a good swimmer."

"Who told you that?" he asked, startled by his own **notoriety**.

"Your counselor from last year. I did some **sleuthing** before you guys got here, to see what I was in for."

Greased Watermelon is a game in which you lubricate a watermelon and essentially play water polo with it. But it's too **ponderous** to throw and it isn't **buoyant** either, so it turns into a giant free-for-all. It's one of those games that is really more for the **amusement** of the counselors.

"Last year at Greased Watermelon," recounted Spencer, "the counselors covered Johnny in butter and put him in a life jacket."

Case in point.

By the time I brought Spencer back to bed, his tears had dried. He and the other boys spent the next couple of days at camp in a little pod of eight-year-old anxiety and **elation**. Gonzalo, who was **gregarious** and only mildly disturbed, was quickly given the nickname Gonzo. Stevie, the **scheming** Greenwich kid, busied himself trying to get everyone else into trouble. He was **deft** at this. And Johnny, with his knock-knees

---

Notoriety: n. the state of being known and talked of widely and unfavorably.
Sleuth: v. to act as a detective; search for information.
Ponderous: adj. very heavy; clumsy because of weight and size.
Buoyant: adj. capable of floating.
Amusement: n. entertainment; pleasurable diversion.
Elation: n. the quality or state of euphoria.
Gregarious: adj. social; liking companionship.
Scheming: adj. devious; plotting.
Deft: adj. skillful; nimble; clever.

and oversize Yankees hat flopping over one ear, became the **shrieking** mascot of the tent. No matter how many times I yanked up his tube socks or told him to tie his shoes, the kid was always **disheveled**.

Shouts of "Uncle Chris!"—or, as Gonzo pronounced it, "Uncle Kreees!"—even **infiltrated** my dreams, allowing me no escape.

To **evade** my campers and the high volume of Tent Three, I turned to "the counselor room." This **asylum** was not much more than a room with a bunch of smelly lockers and beanbag chairs. A pitcher of **noxious** bug juice (appropriately named) sat on the table. In the corner, some couches slumped, pockmarked by burns from cigarettes. Well, maybe not cigarettes. This was part of the mystery **shrouding** the dumpy counselor room. I had been waiting to get inside of it since I was nine years old.

On the second day of camp, while most of the kids **migrated** in a **throng** to the docks for a "free swim," the staff flocked to the counselor room. When I arrived, the room was already full. Guys hung all over the furniture, sitting on the

Shriek: v. to utter a shrill cry.
Disheveled: adj. untidy; unkempt.
Infiltrate: v. to pass into or through.
Evade: v. to escape from; avoid capture by; elude.
Asylum: n. a place of refuge and protection; a secure retreat.
Noxious: adj. physically harmful or destructive to living beings.
Shroud: v. to cover, screen, or guard.
Migrate: v. to move periodically from one region to another.
Throng: n. a crowding together of many persons; a pack of things pressed together.

floor and atop piles of dirty laundry. Everyone looked sweaty and **beleaguered**. You would think some sort of **calamity** had befallen Camp Winona.

"What's going on?" I asked.

"We're never going to survive!" wailed Ross. Ross was the slightly **rotund** arts-and-crafts counselor. We called him Ralph. As in Wiggum.

"I want to die," added Amanda, the ecology counselor, **brooding**. She was the only girl in the unit, and a cute one at that.

"You do not want to *die*," I laughed at her **melodrama**.

"Today a kid pooped in the urinal by the baseball field," she said. "I had to clean it out. *By hand*. Let me want to die if I want to die, OK?"

Bitching and moaning in the counselor room was **cathartic**. After merely ten minutes of **parodying** your wackjob counselees, you were **rejuvenated** for ten more hours of work.

"Oh dear," I said, leaning onto my locker. There was no room on the floor. I scanned the room. None of us, except the unit director and senior counselors, were over the age of twenty-five. We were a bunch of kids in charge of slightly smaller kids.

Beleaguer: v. to trouble; harass.
Calamity: n. an extraordinarily grave event marked by great loss and lasting distress; a great misfortune.
Rotund: adj. round; plump.
Brood: v. to dwell gloomily on a subject.
Melodrama: n. something having a sensational or theatrical quality.
Cathartic: adj. relating to purgation of the emotions.
Parody: v. to imitate in a humorous manner; ridicule.
Rejuvenate: v. to make youthful; renew; refresh.

My cabinmate Karl walked in and greeted us, looking **energetic** and **cherubic**, as always.

"What's with the smiles?" Ross/Ralph shot at him.

"Yeah. You look like an ad for Newport cigarettes," added Alex, **irked** by Karl's **effusive** manner. Alex was the canoe-trips counselor. He was British and therefore cooler than the rest of us. It was all in the accent.

"I just had a good time at soccer," Karl said, shrugging. "Aren't you guys going swimming?"

"Are you kidding?" Amanda moaned. "The monsters are out there!"

"If someone poops in the lake, does Amanda still have to clean it up?" **mused** Alex.

"If a Brit gets murdered in the middle of the woods, will anybody care?" Amanda fired back.

"Um, I'm going for a swim," I said, **deserting** the **irritable** group. I was starting to think Camp Winona had a **specialty** after all: survival of the fittest counselor. My vote was for Karl.

❊

Our unit director was a man by the name of Rob Potter. Called "Potts" by everyone from the campers to his own

Energetic: adj. full of energy; operating with viger.
Cherubic: adj. an innocent-looking usually chubby and rosy person.
Irk: v. to irritate; annoy.
Effusive: adj. expressive of great emotion.
Muse: v. to think or say reflectively.
Desert: v. to abandon; forsake.
Irritable: adj. easily exasperated or annoyed.
Specialty: n. a special characteristic; a distinctive feature or quality.

mother, he was a **potent** figure. Potts was just over six feet tall, built like a tank, and handsome in a surfer kind of way. He had a cracked front **incisor** which only showed when he let loose a **cackling** laugh. If the counselors were adored by the boys, Potts was **deified**.

Potts **doled** out torture and love to his campers in equal measures. He knew just when to gibe them, and just when to give a kid a pat on the back. The nicknames that Potts **bestowed** were usually some combination of this humor and affection. Michael Einhorn was named "Strawberry" because he was, well, fat, red, and freckly, but he wore the name as a badge of honor. He even insisted his **bemused** parents use the name when he returned home in August.

A nickname from Potts was truly special. I was named "Slim Pickins" for my **gaunt** physique. See what I mean?

Potts **officiated** all of our games and activities. One night at dinner, while Potts was keeping the rowdy counselors under control, Ross approached me.

"Hey, Rovzar," he said. "Want to see something funny?"

"Sure. What?"

"Watch Lex."

I looked over at Alex. He was leaning against one of the

Potent: adj. powerful; strong; having authority.
Incisor: n. a front tooth typically adapted for cutting.
Cackle: v. to laugh especially in a harsh or sharp manner.
Deify: v. to make a god of.
Dole: v. to give or distribute as a charity; hand out.
Bestow: v. to convey as a gift.
Bemused: adj. having feelings of tolerant amusement.
Gaunt: adj. excessively thin and angular.
Officiate: v. to act in an official capacity; to administer the rules of a game or sport.

barn doors of the main building, his back to the lake. He looked so **somnolent** I wondered if he might nod off.

"My kids got a hold of some candy," Ross griped to me. "God only knows where they **heisted** it from. But they're going nuts." I continued to watch Alex, detecting some movement in the shrubbery behind him. I got the feeling a **clandestine** operation was about to go down.

Ross continued, "They were seriously bouncing off the walls. So I put them on pants patrol. I told them they had to pants as many people as possible before lights-out."

A small child emerged from the shadows behind Alex, who remained blissfully **oblivious**. Elsewhere in the room I noticed a boy creeping up behind Karl.

Suddenly, Ross blew a whistle beside me.

"Jesus!" I yelped, clutching my **vulnerable** ears.

"PANTS PATROL!" Ross yelled. In a nanosecond, Alex, Karl, Will, and Potts's shorts were around their ankles. The relatively orderly Evening Program erupted into complete **mayhem**. Ross's **minions** attacked everyone in sight.

Potts calmly pulled his lacrosse shorts back up. Alex attempted to do the same but fell over.

"Very funny, Uncle Wiggum," Potts said. "But you know what this means?" Potts appreciated a good prank, but he always got his **vengeance**.

Somnolent: adj. sleepy; drowsy; tending to cause sleep.

Heist: v. to commit armed robbery on; steal.

Clandestine: adj. secretive; surreptitious.

Oblivious: adj. completely unaware.

Vulnerable: adj. susceptible to being assaulted or conquered; open to attack.

Mayhem: n. a state of rowdy disorder.

Minion: n. a servile follower or underling; a subordinate person.

Vengeance: n. punishment inflicted in retaliation for an injury or offense.

Potts leaned down to the four kids that were tugging at his pants for an **encore**, and whispered something to them. His instructions were **inaudible** over the shrieking.

"What's he saying?" Ross asked.

"I don't know," I said, **stupefied** by the action of the last sixty seconds.

It became clear as soon as the kids **swarming** around Potts began to chant: "In-the-lake! In-the-lake! In-the-lake!"

"Ross, take your shoes off," I warned.

"What?"

"Take your *shoes* off!" I yelled.

But it was too late. The **din** of mischievous campers rose like the **sinister** buzz of a bee swarm. Potts pointed at Ross, and the kids **assailed** him, grabbing him by his arms and legs.

Throwing counselors in the lake was a time-honored tradition at Winona. Poor Ross was dragged, clothes and all, down the stairs of the lodge to the lake. I winced as his ass, a little too heavy for twenty **diminutive** boys to handle, slammed on every step.

"It's a beautiful thing, really," Potts said, following the kids down to the lake.

❋

That night, the children of Tent Three were high on something, and it certainly wasn't the Sherlock Holmes book I was

Encore: n. a repeated performance, or additional act.
Inaudible: adj. not able to be heard.
Stupefy: v. to make stupid, groggy, or insensible; to astonish.
Swarm: v. to move or assemble in a crowd.
Din: n. a loud, continued noise.
Sinister: malicious; harmful; ominous.
Assail: v. to attack violently with blows or words.
Diminutive: adj. exceptionally or notably small.

reading to them. They kept interrupting my narration, peppering me with questions about Camp Winona traditions. Now that the campers had Drown-the-Uncle down to a science, they seemed eager to move on to more **intrepid** acts, like Tip-the-Latrine.

"Uncle KREEEES," Gonzo wailed. "What tribe were *you* when you were in Junior?"

"Don't you want to know what happens when Sherlock catches Watson in the Moors with the hound of the Baskervilles?" I asked.

"I think you're making the stories up as you go along," accused Johnny.

"Uncle Krees, tell us about the Old Man Sturdly!" Gonzo whined.

I paused.

"Who told you about Old Man Sturdly?" I asked.

"Johnny did."

"Johnny, how do you know about Old Man Sturdly?"

"I heard some kids talk about it last year. But my counselor wouldn't tell me the stories."

Old Man Sturdly was the **mythological** villain of camp who was **conceived** to keep children **inactive** at night. He had a long wooden bar with forty holes in it, which he tried to fill with the eyeballs of **abducted** Winona campers. He had a mob of **malignant** followers named the Bagamores who lived under a signpost in downtown Bridgton. I kid you not.

Intrepid: adj. resolutely fearless.
Mythological: adj. lacking factual basis or historical validity.
Conceive: v. to originate; cause to begin.
Inactive: adj. idle; sedentary; quiescent.
Abduct: v. to carry off (as a person) by force.
Malignant: adj. threatening danger; deadly or growing worse.

One had to be **circumspect** when telling camp stories because the stories couldn't be untold. Among the counselors there was a preestablished covenant to keep the Sturdly myth alive. You could duck questions and give **elusive** answers, but a counselor could never **dispel** the Old Man Sturdly myth completely. Without Sturdly, we were a little bit less **sovereign** at Camp Winona.

With the eight-year-olds, however, the Sturdly myth was tricky. While my campers were nearly old enough to **scoff** at scary stories, their age also made them as **impressionable** as the Moose Pond sands.

I looked at Spencer. He was staring at me. My **enigmatic** responses were only **whetting** his curiosity.

"I'm sorry, I can't tell you about Old Man Sturdly. But I will someday if you guys are really good."

"Is he real?" Spencer asked in a whisper.

"Oh he's real."

"Have you seen him?" Johnny took his turn **cajoling** me.

"No. But I've heard him."

"You *heard* him?" Gonzo hissed. The boys were **captivated**.

"Yes. That's how you know he's coming. That's why we all

Circumspect: adj. careful of ones behavior; discreet.
Elusive: adj. evading grasp or pursuit; cleverly avoiding.
Dispel: v. to drive off or away; cause to vanish.
Sovereign: adj. possessing supreme power.
Scoff: v. to express scorn, derision, or contempt; mock.
Impressionable: adj. easily influenced.
Enigmatic: adj. mysterious; hard to understand; cryptic.
Whet: v. to excite; stimulate.
Cajole: v. to persuade by flattery, especially in the face of reluctance; gentle urging.
Captivate: v. to influence by some special charm, art, or trait; charm with an irresistible appeal; enchant.

have to be quiet after lights-out. And also, why you need to stay in your tent and not go wandering around. You want to keep your eyes, right?"

"MY EYES?" shrieked Gonzo.

Worried that my answers were actually **exacerbating** the problem, I did what any counselor with half a brain would do. I declared lights-out.

❉

The next morning I woke, as usual, at six, to the sound of Spencer's snuffling. I looked over at Karl, sleeping soundly with his tent full of perfect kids. Damn him.

I got out of bed and sat with Spencer. Our conversations followed a basic, easy script. I was secretly relieved that today's version didn't feature a new character by the name of Sturdly.

"I'm not having fun, Uncle Chris. I think I want to go home," he repeated for the tenth time.

"You've been here less than a week, man. It'll get better, I promise. Don't you believe me?" I mumbled.

"No."

I swear my summer job description had been about wearing hemp bracelets, playing Frisbee golf, and **subsisting** on s'mores. There was no mention of playing shrink with **melancholy** eight-year-olds, and no training for it either. The rest of that day was even worse. My kids **tirelessly** harassed me about Old Man Sturdly. Physically and mentally.

"Ow! No biting, Gonzo!" I yelled.

Exacerbate: v. to irritate; aggravate.
Subsist: v. to exist; remain alive.
Melancholy: adj. sad; pensive; depressed.
Tireless: adj. diligent; untiring.

"I stop biting if you tell us about Old Man Sturdly and the Bagamores," he beseeched, running out of the tent to brush his teeth.

"You'll stop biting if you value your life," I yelled after him. "Bad Gonzo!"

Finally, I **succumbed** to my campers and introduced them to Old Man Sturdly. The only problem was that I got a little carried away with my **narration** and **embellished** the villain at every turn. There were voices. And sound effects. I even added an eyeless witch who lived across the pond. I told them that's why we had a counselor hang out in the grove with the tents every night—so that their eyeballs were not **imperiled**.

"So that's the story," I finished, well after lights–out. "You guys still awake?"

"I never will sleep again," Gonzo said. Everyone laughed. I looked over at Spencer. During the whole story he had been sitting upright in bed, with wide, excited eyes. When Spencer slept through the following morning without bawling, I **deduced** that I had done the right thing. With some thinking outside the box, I just may have cured Tent Three of homesickness. Best counselor ever!

I sat out on the swim docks the next afternoon, watching the kids **flail** around in the water. As a sailing counselor and a

---

Succumb: v. to give way under pressure; yield.
Narration: n. story.
Embellish: v. to heighten the attractiveness of by adding decorative details.
Imperil: v. to put in danger; threaten.
Deduce: v. to infer from a general principle; to derive, as a conclusion.
Flail: v. to wave; swing.

lifeguard, I was **obligated** to supervise. This meant, of course, working on my tan and **catapulting** children into the water. Thank heavens they were **limber**.

"Hey, buttbag," someone said to me as I lay out on my towel. I squinted up. It was Will, the riflery counselor. Will was from my hometown on the coast of Maine—a place that was **quaint**, white, and unforgivably preppy. Will was like the town poster boy, looking like he had just stumbled out of a 1970s yachting catalog. He wore **preposterous** aviators, ribbon belts, and his collars were always turned up.

"Yes, ass hat?" I replied. There had always been **animosity** between us, but now Will was standing in my sun. This was not cool.

"You told your tent about Old Man Sturdly?"

Oops.

"Yeah, why?"

"Because now *my* tent is begging me to hear about it," he said. Will hadn't had much luck in picking tents. He was saddled with Tent One—the very youngest campers. These were **infantile** kids who sucked their thumbs, couldn't focus for more than seven minutes, and **habitually** wet the bed.

"You probably shouldn't tell them. They'll get scared."

"Uh, yeah. Obviously. I'm really glad they're on to it, though," he said, pouring the sarcasm on thick. "Little kids love

---

Obligate: v. to require.
Catapult: v. to throw or launch by or as if by a catapult.
Limber: adj. agile; flexible.
Quaint: adj. pleasingly or strikingly old-fashioned or unfamiliar.
Preposterous: adj. contrary to common sense; utterly absurd.
Animosity: n. ill will or resentment tending toward active hostility; an antagonistic attitude.
Infantile: adj. characteristic of a baby.
Habitual: adj. customary; by habit.

it when you have a secret you won't tell them. Makes them really **sedate**."

"Sorry. It seemed like a good idea at the time."

While my own popularity **plummeted**, the five boys of Tent Three were the hit of Camp Winona for the rest of the day. Every other counselor was immediately **harassed** for details about Old Man Sturdly and his evil **cronies**. It was worth getting a few dirty looks. I was giving my kids precisely what I had spent my summers at Camp Winona **pining** away for: overnight coolness.

"Uncle Kreees?"

Someone was whispering very close to my head. I opened my eyes and found myself staring into the bulb of a flashlight.

"What's going on, Gonzo?" I asked. "What time is it?"

"I don't know. You guys take away my watch at the beginning of the summer."

"Right. What's wrong?"

"I hear something."

"What do you mean you hear something?"

"I hear something outside the cabin."

"Right now?"

"No, a while ago."

"What was it?"

"I don't know. It sound like someone sneak around."

Sedate: adj. keeping a quiet steady attitude or pace.
Plummet: v. to drop sharply and abruptly.
Harass: v. to annoy by repeated attacks; disturb or torment persistently.
Crony: n. a close friend especially of long standing.
Pine: v. to yearn intensely and persistently especially for something unattainable.

"Oh no," I said, realizing what was **afoot**.

"You think it is Old Man Sturdly?" he asked in a hushed tone.

"Is that why you're awake?" I asked. "Are you scared?"

"Yes. I am very scared."

Worst. Counselor. Ever.

"Oh, Gonzo! You begged me to tell that story. Why did you want to hear it if you knew it was going to scare you?"

"I didn't know it was so scary to me like this."

I looked over at Karl, who was now awake. I mouthed "sorry" and he shook his head, his **discountenance** obvious.

"Listen Gonzo, you're safe here. No camper has ever been hurt by Old Man Sturdly. Plus, I'm right here. I won't let anything happen."

I felt like an ass. Who lies to a scared little kid? But those were the rules.

"But you are sleeping."

"Well, I'll wake up. I know what he sounds like. I promise. You have to trust me, OK?"

"OK." Gonzo clearly did not trust me. Apparently, to eight-year-olds, I rank right up there with dental hygienists and strangers **proffering** candy.

"You want me to sit with you while you fall asleep?"

"Yes."

I tucked Gonzo back in and sat with him, rubbing his back until he fell asleep. Somewhere in heaven, I hoped I was racking up **martyr** points. Then I went back to sleep.

The next morning I woke to snuffling. Again. I did my best

Afoot: adv., adj. in the process of development; underway.

Discountenance: n. disfavor; disapproval.

Proffer: v. to offer; put before a person for acceptance.

Martyr: n. a person who sacrifices something of great value and especially life itself for the sake of principle.

to tune it out and fill my head with **soporific** thoughts, **desperate** to sleep through the crying so I wouldn't have to feel so **callous**. After about twenty minutes had passed, I heard movement from the other side of the tent. I lay still.

"Hey Spencer, are you OK?" a voice **inquired**.

It was Johnny. I heard him clomp over to Spencer's bed and climb aboard.

"Spencer, what's wrong?"

"I don't know," Spencer said.

"Do you miss your mom?"

"Yeah, I guess so."

"I miss my mom, too." That was Stevie's voice. He got out of bed, too.

What was going on?

"But I want to go home. You guys are having fun. I'm not," Spencer **bawled**.

"That's not true," Johnny said. "You're having fun, too. It just doesn't seem like it right now—but during the day you have a lot of fun. Like, what are you excited about doing today?"

I opened my eyes wide. Had Johnny nabbed my script?

"I don't know. I guess archery," Spencer said. He had stopped crying.

"Was that your favorite thing from last summer?" Stevie asked.

I was **bewildered**.

They went on for ten minutes this way, repeating parts of

Soporific: adj. causing sleep.
Desperate: adj. driven by despair; having an urgent need or desire.
Callous: adj. being hardened and thickened; feeling no sympathy for others.
Inquire: v. to ask (about); seek knowledge (of).
Bawl: v. to shout clamorously; cry vehemently; wail.
Bewilder: v. to confuse; perplex.

the **monologue** they had heard me deliver to Spencer every morning since the beginning of camp. They hadn't been asleep at all. I snuck a peek at the **triumvirate**. Stevie and Johnny had their arms around Spencer, who was smiling, a little embarrassed at the attention, but also **basking** in it. Stevie and Johnny promised to teach Spencer how to play four square during free time, and then they all went back to sleep. Apparently, my terrifying ghost stories had **cultivated** some sort of **solidarity** among my counselees. Old Man Sturdly had been the **catalyst** in bringing these little buggers together.

The following night, once all of my campers had slipped into **profound** sleep, I snuck out. It was the first Saturday night of our summer, and some of the counselors were building a bonfire in a field in the woods. When I got there, people were already **ensconced** in lawn chairs around the fire. I had almost a decade of summers with these guys, back when they were hyperactive boys, **propagating** monster myths and pantsing everyone within reach.

Now, watching them from across the orange fire, it struck me how **tranquil** we seemed. After only a week in **rambunctious**

Monologue: n. a long talk by a single speaker.
Triumvirate: n. any group or set of three.
Bask: v. to take pleasure or derive enjoyment; to lie in a pleasant atmosphere.
Cultivate: v. to foster the growth of; to promote the development of.
Solidarity: n. unity based on common interests, objectives, and standards.
Catalyst: n. an agent that provokes or speeds significant change or action.
Profound: adj. thorough; complete; deep.
Ensconce: v. to establish, to settle in.
Propagate: v. to spread; disseminate.
Tranquil: adj. calm; serene; undisturbed.
Rambunctious: adj. boisterous; unruly.

Tent Three, our maturity felt **tangible**. Camp Winona would never be the same again, but I never wished it to be. Once you become a counselor, sure, there's no such thing as Old Man Sturdly anymore. But there's also no such thing as lights–out, either. We watched the sun come up.

❊ **Chris Rovzar** went to high school in Maine and attended Yale University. He rowed on the crew team and wrote for the daily newspaper. Since college, Chris has been working as a gossip columnist for the *New York Post*, which involves attending parties on a nightly basis. Chris highly recommends this type of work.

Tangible: adj. definite or concrete; capable of being identified.

5

CONFESSIONS OF A VAGABOND SWIMMER

Arianne Cohen

As a freshman, my living requirements were simple: a happy home near a good swim team and a good high school. After all, I'd lived in the same place for the previous fourteen years—a house located hours from the pool, and minutes from a terrible junior high—and I was a bit bored. I knew every creak of every floorboard, not to mention the life stories of every retiree in my neighborhood. Living with new folk in a new place would be exciting. Stimulating. Engaging.

My mom drove me down to Pennsylvania the summer before ninth grade and dropped me and my suitcases at the home of Family #1. Competitive swimming is an intense sport, with a **requisite** four hours of daily training. Few schools run **adequately** intense programs, and the closest was five hours down the highway in suburban Pennsylvania. Perfect. The team was called Foxcatcher, and known for placing swimmers on the Olympic team. A handful of kids from around the country lived nearby with host families, attending the regular high school attached to the team. This arrangement may sound weird, but when one is already training five hours a day, such

Requisite: adj. required; necessary.
Adequate: adj. sufficient; suitable.

provisional measures help normalize things, by putting your pool in the same building as your school, and giving you hundreds of teammates with the same **agenda**.

After dropping me off, my mom cried all the way home. Meanwhile, I was pumped. This would be an amazing adventure. No rules! I would be living with a single mother and her six-year-old daughter Ashley in a big house, next door to a Foxcatcher swimmer.

That first night, I unpacked my bags, ate dinner with the mother–daughter pair, and went to sleep. Ashley seemed a bit hyperactive, breaking some dishes while jumping up and down in search of dessert, but I figured she was just **enthralled** by her new houseguest. Little kids are weird sometimes.

The next morning at 5:30 A.M., the swimmer next door picked me up for morning practice. Training in those first weeks was a matter of sheer survival, defined by me running out of steam an hour into practice, and holding on for dear life for the remaining four hours. Midway through, I'd **punctuate** the time by **scampering** past the coaches into the bathroom, where I'd sit on a bench and watch the water drip off the tip of my nose and splat onto the tiles below, trying to convince myself that I would survive the rest of the workout. I sat in a chlorinated **stupor**. A knock would predictably echo off the metal lockers, followed by Coach shrieking, "AAARRRIIIIAAANNNNE? WHAT ARE YOU DOING?!", sending me running back into the pool.

Periodically, former team members and Olympians, now

Provisional: adj. conditional; temporary.
Agenda: n. plan of things to be done; items of business.
Enthrall: v. to captivate; charm.
Punctuate: v. to break into or interrupt at intervals.
Scamper: v. to run quickly and playfully.
Stupor: n. state of extreme apathy; daze.

graying with children, would appear on deck to visit the head coach. They no longer seemed to view the coach as a source of physical pain. I'd stare at them, reminding myself that they were living proof that it was possible to survive training. I, too, might live to adulthood. I stood in the shallow end staring at the successful high school graduates, thinking of all the possibilities I could have if I just lived until 6 P.M. for the next four years. A coach shrieking, "AAARRRIIIIAAANNNNE? WHAT ARE YOU DOING?!", broke my concentration. I plopped my head back underwater and took a few strokes, falling into a pattern with the swimmers in my lane.

I successfully survived that morning, as well as the next two days of training.

On the third day, I returned home at 6 P.M. to find Ashley going bonkers. During dinner she ran through the house **shrieking**, "MOMMY DOESN'T LOVE ME ANYMORE!!!", **lamenting** hysterically. The next night she trashed her room, including overturning her bookshelf, leaving *Curious George* and *Where the Wild Things Are* in a mangled heap. This was quickly followed by an unfortunate **episode** involving Ashley and two gallons of house paint in the basement.

On day six, her **bedraggled** mother came into my bedroom while her daughter screeched a **diatribe** against bedtime in the background, to calmly inform me that she would have to evict me. She was **apologetic**. Everyone's family, I figured, had issues; Ashley's were just particularly **visible**. I packed my bags.

Shriek: v. to yell in a shrill outcry.
Lament: v. to express sorrow (for); mourn; bewail.
Episode: n. an incident in a series of events; one happening.
Bedraggled: adj. unkempt; in a state of deterioration; untidy.
Diatribe: n. a bitter and abusive speech.
Apologetic: adj. expressing regret.
Visible: adj. on view.

The swim team scrambled to find me a new home, **promptly** placing me with Family #2, the Kallozis. Their daughter Monica was my age, and since it was summer, we stayed up late at night watching movies like *Interview with the Vampire*, which we both viewed from behind the couch, peering over the cushions to **ascertain** whether it was OK to look. (It wasn't.)

During the days, we swam. If high school social groups are cliques, then swim teams are **veritable** cults. You have to prove yourself, both physically and socially, before anyone will talk to you, a **feat** that would take my awkward self around six months to achieve. Until then, I lived in a social **quarantine**. I talked with Monica and the kids my age, but generally steered clear of the juniors, seniors, and college swimmers, a handful of whom were world champions, instead listening quietly to the locker room buzz about sex and parties and drinking and all sorts of activities in which I was not nearly cool enough to **partake**.

One day I unknowingly committed social suicide by choosing to sit in the backseat when a senior came and picked me up for swim practice. I walked into the locker room just in time to hear her say, "Arianne thinks I'm her freaking *chauffeur*." I buried my face in my towel, and determined that I would never talk to anyone again, and always sit in the front seat.

I remained **oblivious** to Mrs. Kallozi's assumption that I would be living with her temporarily, "for a few days." Nine

Prompt: adj. quick to act; performed immediately.
Ascertain: v. to find out by examination; determine.
Veritable: adj. true; genuine.
Feat: n. an act of remarkable skill or valor.
Quarantine: n. a period of enforced seclusion, usually to prevent contagion.
Partake: v. to participate; take part in.
Oblivious: adj. unaware; lacking knowledge of.

weeks later, the summer was over, and Mrs. Kallozi knew that she couldn't manage her own full-time nurse's schedule with an additional child. I was once again **evicted**.

This turned out to be **fortuitous**, because three weeks after I left, Monica ran away from home to Florida by booking a flight with her parents' credit card. The Kallozi's marriage fell apart weeks later. Thus, I had successfully **skirted** a major **maelstrom**. But I was still homeless, and risking a return to the boring house of my youth.

So I moved again, to my third family in twelve weeks, this time into the home of the Laohaphans, a Thai family of two parents and their son, a swimmer named Timmy. I was now **adept** at moving, having trimmed down my belongings to two suitcases, **discarding** such items as a lawn chair (for summer swim meets) and a **gargantuan** pot (for macaroni and cheese).

Honestly, I didn't mind the moving. Each time, I threw my shirts, pants, and school supplies into the new empty drawers, not yet owning enough important possessions to care. And I still felt that my new life was an **escapade** of adventure.

The only problem at this point was that I'd **resided** in four homes in twelve weeks, and I could no longer find the spoon drawer if you paid me. Kitchen organization **schemes** tend to blend together, and I would regularly stand in the middle of the

Evict: v. to expel; kick out.
Fortuitous: adj. fortunate; lucky; happening by lucky chance.
Skirt: v. to pass along the border of; go around in order to avoid.
Maelstrom: n. a whirlpool; a tumultuous state of affairs.
Adept: adj. skillful; expert.
Discard: v. to cast off; reject; throw away as useless.
Gargantuan: adj. enormous; gigantic.
Escapade: n. a foolish or wild adventure.
Reside: v. to dwell or live in.
Scheme: n. a regular or formal plan; a system.

Laohaphan kitchen, hopelessly trying to **channel** the location of the spatulas or the sugar. Sometimes I would ask myself, If I were Mrs. Laohaphan, where would I put the knives? The **strategy** rarely worked. On my visits home to my mother, I'd stare at her desk, trying to telepathically find the stamps.

A few things struck me as odd at my new home. I moved into a bedroom at the end of the hall, while all three Laohaphans lived in the same room on the other end of the hall, sleeping in the same bedroom. The rest of the house—two more bedrooms, and an entire lower level—remained furnished, but **vacant**.

Meanwhile, Timmy and his father were gun **fanatics**, frequently **embarking** on weekend trips to shooting ranges. I was informed of this when I walked past their bedroom on my first night in the house, to see them perched on the queen-size bed, cleaning their guns. I didn't quite know what to make of this, but my new teammates **assured** me they were fully licensed, as did Timmy, so I let it go.

Silence often ruled the home, **interspersed** with the **drone** of televisions and radios. Mr. Laohaphan and Mrs. Laohaphan did not speak to each other. They hadn't spoken in years. Instead, they communicated through Timmy, who translated back and forth for them in varying Thai and English. ("Dad, Mom needs some money." "Mom, Dad wants to know where the car wash is.") As a couple, they had lost all respect for each other, leading Mr. Laohaphan to ignore Mrs. Laohaphan, and Mrs. Laohaphan to cry.

Channel: v. to transmit; send from one person or place to another.
Strategy: n. a careful method or plan.
Vacant: adj. empty; having no contents.
Fanatic: a zealot, esp. in religion.
Embark: v. to set out; make a start.
Assure: v. to make sure or certain; make secure or stable.
Intersperse: v. to insert among other things.
Drone: n. a monotonous, continuous sound, often buzzing, humming, or murmuring.

Yet, the first lesson of living with other people's families is to keep your head down. None of these matters were my business, so I ignored them, periodically throwing in a sympathetic nod for both sides. Besides, I was fully occupied with five daily hours of swim practice, plus a full academic schedule at a new school, for which I'd been **defectively** prepared by my old school. And, with my free time, I could have fully **engaged** myself figuring out how to pronounce "Lao-hap-han." I successfully lived in a bubble, **emerging** only on hilly car rides with Mrs. Laohaphan, who would drive in circles, and tell me how badly she wanted to return to Thailand, and how she didn't have any friends and how she missed her family and how she spent much of her time sitting downstairs crying. I encouraged her to go home. But she didn't want to leave Timmy. So she stayed.

Sometimes a Laohaphan parent would take Timmy and me to the grocery store, in an effort to figure out what I wanted to eat (I didn't know, my mom had always bought stuff), with Timmy blasting the new James Bond theme song from the cassette player on repeat. This was the extent of our family bonding.

In the evenings, Mrs. Laohaphan cooked Thai **fare** that I didn't like, and brought it up to the bedroom for Timmy and her husband. I sat at the kitchen table **scrutinizing** *Beverly Hills 90210* reruns for **morsels** of advice on how to be cool, while eating three or four bowls of Lucky Charms cereal for dinner. **Periodically**, the Laohaphans creaked the floorboards

Defective: adj. imperfect; broken.
Engage: v. to involve; gain the attention of.
Emerge: v. to appear; come into view from something that conceals, especially water.
Fare: n. 1. food served; 2. price charged to transport a person.
Scrutinize: v. to observe or investigate closely.
Morsel: n. a small piece or bit, especially of food.
Periodic: adj. recurring at regular intervals.

of their room above, signaling their **resituating** themselves around one another. Years later, I lived in Southeast Asia, and learned that Asian cultures commonly live in small spaces and share sleeping quarters. In high school, I just thought that the Laohaphans didn't like being alone.

I talked to my mom daily on the phone, and I told her that things were great. She spent time harping about my freshman grades, which were less than **stellar**.

No one really **monitored** my schedule or goings on—I could, for the most part, come and go as I pleased if I talked someone into giving me a ride. My mom would say "Go to sleep!," and I would hang up the phone and go to a friend's house. But the thing about swimmers is that they just don't have enough time to get in trouble. By the time we were done swimming, we were too exhausted to plan **covert** gatherings or sneak out at night. Really, we just wanted to **hibernate** dryly.

I was doing just that one winter day at the Laohaphans', sleeping off a long week of school and snowstormy **commutes**, when I awoke at dinnertime to find no one home at 7 P.M. on Sunday night. They were out at a Thai party, and would be back after dinner. There was nothing to do. None of my friends were around. I poured myself some cereal and flipped through television channels. Nothing. I went upstairs and looked through my bookshelf—eh, nothing. I wandered into the garage, and spotted the car: their blue Toyota. This is

Resituate: v. to rearrange in a particular place.
Stellar: adj. 1. outstanding; 2. relating to the stars.
Monitor: v. to keep track of.
Covert: adj. secret; hidden.
Hibernate: v. to be inactive or asleep; pass the winter in seclusion and resting, as bears and some animals do.
Commute: v. to travel daily back and forth.

the moment when fourteen-year-olds get into trouble: on a **mundane** school night, when there's nothing better to do.

Of course! I could play with the car! That would be **engaging**, more fun than eating cereal and watching the news.

I ran upstairs to grab the extra keys and flip-flops, and jumped behind the wheel. I had never driven a car before, and had no clue how the thing worked. I turned the key, and felt the engine roar to life. To get out, I would have to slide backward. I hit the garage-door button above my head, looked down at the gear shift, roll it into R, and lowered the parking brake.

I **eased** my foot off the brake, and the car jerked backward all by itself. This was unexpected. I slammed the brake and sat still. My heart was racing. Well, I guess that had gone OK.

I picked my foot up again, very gently, and the car slowly rolled backward, the back tires hitting the driveway, moving no more than a centimeter a second. I watched my progress through the rearview mirror. Success! Rolling backward, rolling backward, rolling backward.

I was halfway out of the garage. I glanced toward the front and squinted to notice that I was very close to the left wall. Wait, the car was somehow at a diagonal angle. A **mammoth** scraping shook the right side of the car, spurring my foot onto the brake, just in time to hear a strange popping sound.

I froze. This was not good.

I pulled up the parking break, turned off the car, undid my seat belt and walked around the back of the car.

As my flip-flop hit the pavement, I slid a bit, and realized what had happened: The car had hit black ice, an **insidious**

Mundane: adj. ordinary; commonplace; usual.
Engaging: adj. attracting of attention; intriguing.
Ease: v. to lessen pressure; to free from something.
Mammoth: adj. gigantic; immense.
Insidious: adj. subtle but with evil effect; seemingly harmless but actually damaging; harmful but enticing.

norm on Pennsylvania roads, and **skated** backward on an angle. The car hadn't been **deployed** by gas at all, but instead slid sideways on ice. The right hood of the car was pressed up against the doorway of the garage, the side mirror broken and hanging off the car. The back of the car touched the bushes along the garage.

I had broken the Laohaphans' car. Shoot. This was not good. My heartbeat hit "I'm in serious trouble" mode.

I ran upstairs and thought about who I could call, someone who might be able to **convey** how to move the car and hide the **destruction**. Not my mom—she would freak. But I needed a driver. I called the swim-team captain, a girl named Tracey who **barely** knew who I was, but seemed nice and knew how to drive.

She didn't know me because my **primary** social purpose on the swim team was as Team Jew. My duties as Team Jew were as follows:

- Address all queries about Jews, Jewishness, and Judaism.
- Inform teammates of holiday traditions.
- Keep my **agnostic** preferences a secret.

As such, I quickly became the go-to person for all things Jewish, fielding a steady flow of **queries** like, "Why do you

Skate: v. to glide or roll.
Deploy: v. to move strategically or appropriately.
Convey: v. to communicate; impart.
Destruction: n. a scene of ruin.
Barely: adv. scarcely; hardly.
Primary: adj. first; principal; of most importance.
Agnostic: n. a person who believes that the existence of God is unknowable.
Query: n. a question; an inquiry.

guys always get two days off right near the beginning of the school year? That's not fair!" "Is it true that you don't eat on holidays?" My first Hannukah involved an enormous HAPPY HANNUKAH sign **strung** across my swim locker. My locker-mate was very pleased with herself.

Tracey was only loosely aware of this **expertise**:

"Hello?"

"This is Arianne."

"Who?"

"Arianne Cohen. I am on the swim team."

"Who?"

"Arianne. Team Jew."

"Oh . . . hi."

"Um, I was wondering if you could help me."

"OK."

"Well, I was just trying to drive, and I crashed the Lao-haphans' car into the side of their garage."

There was a pause. "Did you tell the Laohaphans?"

"They're not home."

"Oh."

"So I was wondering if you can explain to me how to un-crash the car?"

"Um, it's up against the garage?"

"Yeah."

"You're screwed."

My stomach plunged.

"Do you have prayers for this? Maybe God could help."

I didn't have any prayers at all, let alone a "The Laopahhans' Car Is Stuck on the Garage" prayer. But Tracey had made it clear that she couldn't really help me. But she **elucidated** how

---

String: v. to hang.
Expertise: n. specialized skill or knowledge; know-how.
Elucidate: v. to make clear; explain.

to move the car into first gear, the number 1, and that maybe I could move forward and at least repark the car, to **ameliorate** the visual **atrocity**.

I ran back downstairs. I'd left the garage door open, and the entire first-floor temperature was **glacial**. I restarted the car, but had to wait a moment because I was shaking. I put on my seat belt, lowered the safety brake, and moved the shift until the red highlighted 1.

I took a deep breath and slowly lifted my foot off the brake. The car moved forward just a bit, with a loud cranking side from the right. I bit my lip and persevered. The crank turned into a crumbling noise, the sound of metal being **irreplaceably** bent against a garage-door track. I hit the brake, stopped the car, and got back out. Two thirds of the car was hanging out of the garage, with the tail of the car now fully in the bushes at a forty-five degree angle with the garage. It appeared that the car was quite stuck against the garage door, and that any further movement would just scrape up the side of the car more. I stood behind the car and attempted to use my swimming muscles to lift the rear of the car, straining until my biceps hurt. The car didn't **budge**.

I looked at the clock. The Laohaphans would be home soon. Tracey couldn't help me, and neither could the good Lord.

I went upstairs and sat on my bed for a while to think. I was afraid of Mr. Laohaphan. He owned a gun and would be **apoplectic** to find that he no longer owned two functional cars.

Ameliorate: v. to make better; improve.
Atrocity: n. an appalling, horrifying, or wicked state.
Glacial: adj. pertaining to ice or glaciers.
Irreplaceable: adj. not replaceable.
Budge: v. to move; stir.
Apoplectic: adj. greatly excited or angered; causing a stroke.

I considered running away before he got home, but it was frigging cold outside, and I didn't have anywhere to go in Pennsylvania. Besides, my mom would *not* be thrilled to see me. My only option was to go to sleep. I reached into my book bag and pulled out a piece of loose-leaf paper, on which I wrote a note:

> *Dear Mr. and Mrs. Laohaphan,*
>
> *I was driving the car, and now it is stuck. I am very sorry. I am going to sleep now. I am very sorry. I will talk with you in the morning. I am very sorry.*
>
> *Arianne*

I went back downstairs, and **gazed** again at the car. This was a disaster. I taped the note to the windshield of the car, and **retreated** to my bedroom, locking the door behind me. Then I climbed into my bed, pulled two comforters over my head, and curled my knees under my abdomen.

❁

Two hours later, I heard their car roll into the driveway, and then heard a lot of voices. All three voices, presumably **inquiring** why their car was crumpled against the garage doorway, half in the bushes.

I continued hiding, tensing up my entire body. There were so many voices that I wondered if Mr. and Mrs. L. were actually speaking to each other. Perhaps my crashing their car could be their **reconciliation**. I heard footsteps in the hallway

---

Gaze: v. to look at intently.
Retreat: v. to go back; run from an enemy.
Inquire: v. to ask about; seek knowledge (of).
Reconciliation: n. a restored union or friendship.

and froze. Timmy's voice yelled down to his parents, "Yeah, she's asleep!" The footsteps **departed**.

There was silence, and then I heard the car engine rev up. The engine **idled**, and then an enormous *craaank* sound echoed through the house, **reverberating** the wall my bed lay against. I winced, pressing my face into the mattress.

I could hear the car idling, then moving, then idling, then silence. There were more voices, a car door slam, and the sounds of all three Laohaphans' footsteps padding into their bedroom. The door closed behind them. Silence.

I moved my head out from under the covers. Maybe things would turn out OK. Mr. Laohaphan hadn't gone after me with his gun. Maybe they moved the car, the car was miraculously unharmed, I would survive the next three and a half years of swim practices, and everything would be **copacetic**. I closed my eyes, but was far too wound up to sleep. I turned on the television, and watched David Letterman on mute.

I heard Mrs. Laohaphan's feet moving down the hallway and toward the kitchen. I thought for a minute. This would be my chance. Mrs. Laohaphan didn't know how to use guns. I could talk to her.

I quietly opened my door, and walked barefoot down to the kitchen.

She looked up at me. "Why you wreck car?"

The tears started streaming before I opened my mouth to release a **litany** of apologies. "I am so *so* sorry. I was just trying to play with it and then I hit the ice and then there was

---

Depart: v. to go or move away; leave.
Idle: v. to operate while not connected; do nothing.
Reverberate: v. to reflect sound; continuously echo.
Copacetic: adj. satisfactory.
Litany: n. a sizeable series; a lengthy recitation.

screeching and I am so so sorry and I will pay to have the car fixed." I started to bawl.

"You will pay?"

"Yes."

"OK." She nodded at me and returned a bowl of fruit to the refrigerator. She somehow seemed **contented** with this turn of events.

I didn't quite understand what had **transpired**, but I returned to my room, and she returned to hers.

The next day, the entire swim team knew about the car **incident** by 7 A.M. I decided to **revert** to my **tactic** of **refraining** from talking. Meanwhile, Timmy helpfully **recounted** the story with **glee**, including the line, "Why you wreck car?", which quickly gained popularity among the boys' team. They liked to shriek the phrase across the pool deck in my direction, as in "Arrriannne, why you wreck caaa?"

My stomach **churned** as I evaded conversation all day, **dodging** questions on why I wrecked the car, and where I had been going. But I hadn't been going anywhere. I was just going to stay in the driveway. And play with the car. Or something.

I kept my **explication** to "I dunno." I couldn't tell the swim team that I'd moved the car four yards and had a major crash.

That afternoon, as I paddled up the pool, I heard the

Contented: adj. satisfied; placidly happy.
Transpire: v. to happen; occur.
Incident: n. an occurrence or event; a happening.
Revert: v. to go back to a former place, position, or state; return.
Tactic: n. a method or device for accomplishing an end.
Refrain: v. to hold oneself back; abstain.
Recount: v. to tell; relate; narrate in order.
Glee: n. mirth; delight.
Churn: v. to agitate; experience violent motion.
Dodge: v. to evade; avoid a duty or object.
Explication: n. a clarification; an explanation.

"AARRRRRIIIIIAAANNNNNE!!!" from underwater. My coach had just found out about the crash. I got to explain to him, too, why I'd wrecked the car ("I dunno.") and where I had been going ("Nowhere.").

He turned a shade of **mauve** when I told him that I went to sleep after I crashed the car, and his forehead **pulsed** purple when he learned that I hadn't yet **related** the events to my mom. He **supervised** my call. She, too, had a lot of questions. ("You did *what*?" "*Where* were you going?" "Are you a *moron*?")

I just kept promising that I'd pay for it. That seemed to be the **retort** that everyone wanted to hear, so I repeated it a lot. I had no idea how large the **expenditure** might be for a garage-crumpled car. I knew I had **hoarded** years of birthday-gift funding. I decided not to ask. It turned out that fourteen years of birthday savings **precisely** covers the cost of a side-ways car crash.

My coach eventually let me dive back into the pool, to lose myself in the **anonymity** of ten other swimmers in my lane. I tried to forget the incident, but swim teams have long memories, and the **phrase** "Why you wreck caaaa?" came to greet me at every salutation for four years. The phrase was in use long after anyone could remember the details of its **origin**.

Mauve: adj. a color or dye, moderate purple or lilac.
Pulse: v. to pulsate; throb.
Relate: v. to tell; narrate.
Supervise: v. to oversee; be in charge of.
Retort: n. a quick, witty, or sharp reply.
Expenditure: n. an act of expending something; a spending.
Hoard: v. to amass; save; keep piling up.
Precise: adj. exactly defined; definite; accurate.
Anonymity: n. lacking a name or identity.
Phrase: n. 1. a short, pithy expression; 2. a sequence of words that is not a sentence.
Origin: n. a source; a point of beginning.

The next day, Mrs. Laohaphan drove the car to the shop, while I sat in the passenger seat, **clutching** the dangling side-view mirror with my right hand, my arm soaked with rain. My host family did not consider the crashing of their car a **transitory** event. Host families, it seems, remember when you take their expensive belongings and **annihilate** them. Thus, I needed to move again, this time to the Spear family, with whom I happily stayed for the **outstanding** three years. Blessedly, the Spears did not have any swimmers among them, so no one told them about the car incident. The Spears frequently left their cars in their garage unmonitored, keys hanging on the hooks, unaware of the auto **perpetrator** living under their roof.

✳ **Arianne Cohen** went to high school in Fort Washington, Pennsylvania, where she survived approximately 5,500 hours of swim practices before attending Harvard University. Her broken car experience inspired her first book, *Help, It's Broken!: A Fix-It Bible for the Repair-Impaired*. She now spends her days (and nights, and early mornings) writing books and articles in Manhattan. She does not drive.

Clutch: v. to grab with the hands.
Transitory: adj. lasting only for a time; fleeting.
Annihilate: v. to destroy utterly; reduce to nothing.
Outstanding: adj. not paid or settled; remaining.
Perpetrator: n. a person guilty of committing a crime.

6

CONFESSIONS OF A RUNNING DISASTER

Tom Miller

In September of 1995, the eleven members of my high school cross-country team—seven varsity, four junior varsity—lined up on a concrete dock next to a pond. The seniors said it was for a group photo, and carried with them a disposable camera. Once we were all in place, one of them let out a banshee shriek, before yelling, "*Whoohooo!!* Now we throw the freshman in the pond!" They turned toward me.

"Ha! Good one," I said.

I can't account for the next three seconds of my life, but our **conscripted** photographer seems to have captured it perfectly. In his snapshot, I am airborne, bent slightly at the waist, legs **splayed**, arms **akimbo**. I'm grinning **fatuously**, as if I've just said something obvious—"Golly, gee, water!" or "Look! A fish." I look like the biggest dork in the world.

Only as I was **extricating** myself from the pond, to my

Conscripted: adj. compulsory, required, obligatory.
Splayed: adj. spread out or apart, especially limbs or fingers.
Akimbo: adv. bent arms or legs, with the elbow or knee pointing outward.
Fatuous: adj. silly and pointless.
Extricate: v. to free from something problematic.

teammates' **raucous** laughter, did I realize I had been pushed by six or seven pairs of hands. I struggled onto the **embankment**, wiped the **viscous** scum of algae off my face, and thought two things: I would be captain in three years. And when I was, freshmen wouldn't be hurled into the pond like fishing tackle.

Three years later, I was indeed captain, and my **benign** leadership came as a disappointment to my teammate Adam Van-Weelden. He was our No. 3 runner and had also been thrown in the pond the previous year. "You remember how much *you* hated it?" I asked.

"Shoot—that was funny," he said. *"Please?"*

"No. No freshman-tossing."

Adam obeyed—kind of. Instead of pitching our novices into the pond, he **stealthily** ran up behind them every day in practice and threw them into hedges, pine trees, or oncoming traffic—whatever was handy.

It was actually my second year as captain. I had taken over the previous September, following the suspension of our old captain, senior Brad Groff. Brad was gifted: a three-time conference champ, fourth in the state meet his junior year, physique like a Greek god. He **cultivated** our team's **eccentric** side. Once, he bought a jumbo variety-pack of polyester holiday socks from Target, which had pumpkins and hearts and Christmas trees printed on them, and sported a different pair at

---

Raucous: adj. making loud noise.

Embankment: n. a raised structure used especially to hold back water or to carry a roadway.

Viscous: adj. sticky; thick.

Benign: adj. harmless, gentle.

Stealthily: adv. moving quietly and cautiously, to avoid being seen or heard.

Cultivate: v. to develop and improve.

Eccentric: adj. peculiar; irregular; odd.

each meet. He wore war paint. He ran stoned. While we stretched before meets, he blasted his favorite album, *Psychedelic Surf Groove*, by Common Sense, a Californian reggae group, on infinite loop on his boom box. His favorite song was "Keep It Up," a **languid** number that was, in fact, as I recall, largely **comprised** of the phrase "Keep it up" ("Keep it up / Ja, man, just keep it up. / Keep it up (ja) up (ja) up (ja) / Ja, man, keep it up doodley-oh-oh-oh-oh. / Keep it up.")

Other teams gave us plenty of space. Spectators became **skittish**. When they saw us on training runs, pedestrians crossed to the other side of the street. The only people who didn't shy away were three middle school kids who chased us screaming down the street every afternoon while we ran our warm-ups. They never came very close (there were fifteen of us) and we mostly thought they were funny. Mostly. Then one day, as they were chasing us, one of them yelled, "Yeah, that's it—run you homos! RUN!" and another one started singing "Keep It Up." Brad spun around, **traversed** the fifty yards separating us in six seconds, and hoisted one of the kids right off his feet.

"*What* did you say?" he screamed into the kid's face. "*What* did you say?" The kid quickly saw the **rancor** in Brad's eyes and all those bulging muscles—Brad ran shirtless—and thought he was going to die. He squealed like a pig and began thrashing. After a long moment, Brad **sneered** and tossed him to the ground.

Psychedelic: adj. relating to hallucination (usually drug-induced).
Languid: adj. slow and relaxed.
Comprise: v. to consist of, to be made up of.
Skittish: adj. nervous, restlessly active, jumpy.
Traverse: v. to travel across or through.
Rancor: n. bitterness; hatred.
Sneer: n. a scornful smirk, with one side of the lip raised; a mean smile.

The kid lay half on the curb, half on someone's front lawn, **squalling** and sobbing. The rest of the team started running slowly onward, casting looks of **chagrin** over their shoulders, but the kid kept wailing. I finally backtracked to see if he was hurt. I was a lifeguard, and had been trained that when some-one screams out in pain, you investigate.

"You OK?" I asked the kid.

"Somebody's gonna *pay*!" he said. "Somebody's gonna pay for that!"

"You're not hurt?" I asked. "You can walk?"

"Get the hell away from me!" the kid screamed. He picked up the can of soda he'd been carrying and threw it at my head. Well, what an ungrateful little punk, I thought. But I was all alone with him and his friends.

"What's going on out there?" shouted a woman, who had come out of the house in front of us. The injured kid whined at her **incoherently**—"innocent," "**unprovoked** attack," "some-one's gonna pay."

"What, are you like the track team?" the woman asked. "Who did this?" I wondered if she could identify me in a po-lice lineup. "Listen, I know *you* didn't do anything. But who did?" If I sprinted to the end of the block and turned the cor-ner, she'd lose sight of me. I could be back at school in three minutes. "Look kid—that was a crime. You just witnessed a crime. What was the guy's name?"

I couldn't **denounce** a running mate. My loyalties were to

Squall: v. to cry loudly and continuously, such as a child or injured animal.

Chagrin: n. distress or embarrassment at having failed.

Incoherent: adj. noncomprehensible; lacking clarity.

Provoke: v. to purposely prompt someone to response, usually to deliber-ately cause anger or annoyance.

Denounce: v. to publicly declare something or someone wrong or evil.

the team. I'd be **steadfast**. I **summoned** up my courage, turned my back to her and heard my own **resolute** voice say, "I won't tell you his name was Brad Groff."

The kid's family didn't press criminal charges, but our principal suspended Brad from the team for three weeks, effective immediately. I waited for someone to confront me for turning in Brad, but no one knew. Somehow, no one had noticed that I wasn't with them. They didn't even suspect. We had a team meeting the next day to discuss the **implications** of the suspension.

"This is a **trivial** incident that got blown totally out of proportion," said Coach Blaha, a **diminutive**, endlessly **optimistic** man, who always spoke from behind a pair of wraparound sunglasses.

He considered himself a wisecrack **sage**, coining little **aphorisms** like, "Do unto others as you think they want you to do unto them." But today, he spared us the **maxims**. "Brad's not allowed to practice with us while he's suspended. I'd like Tom to take over as captain. Regardless of where he finishes on this team, we all trust and respect him. He'll lead by example like he always does."

Brad was at the meeting, dressed in a sweater and a pair of heavy leather dress shoes with Hannukah menorah socks.

Steadfast: adj. firm and unwavering, resolute.
Summon: v. to gather up to the surface.
Resolute: adj. determined and unwavering, steadfast.
Implication: n. the conclusion or consequence of something, the resulting meaning.
Trivial: adj. unimportant, of little value, minor.
Diminutive: adj. extremely small.
Optimistic: adj. hopeful, confident and upbeat about the future.
Sage: n. profoundly wise person.
Aphorism: n. a short statement of a principle, often witty; an adage.
Maxim: n. short statement of a rule or truth; a proverbial saying.

"Congrats," Brad said to me. "You'll do OK. Just don't screw up the team while I'm gone. This is, like, my life, man."

Despite my slow **canter** and unimpressive finishes, I held the team together just fine. We joked and cut corners and ran too close to the girls' team, as usual. When Brad came back, we expected it to be just like old times, but he had become **solitary** and often **brooded**. He stretched by himself. He didn't join in when we made fun of Adam's haircut. He clashed with Coach Blaha over tactics. Brad ignored his advice and looked **despondent**. When he won the sectional meet and qualified for state, the *Milwaukee Journal-Sentinel* ran a picture of him under its "Runners to Watch" section. Brad's father made laminated copies of it and passed one out to each of us.

Coach drove the van to Wisconsin Rapids for state. Brad sat next to him. I sat in the back, along with a couple of other guys who weren't running, but wanted to watch. We entertained ourselves by throwing a tennis ball against the backs of the front seats. Brad ignored us and held onto his boom box for dear life. With *Psychedelic Surf Groove* on infinite loop, he began to mellow, but then the batteries died. Coach began talking strategy, the same plan he had been pushing on Brad all season long—go out slow, then **annihilate** the front-runners over the last mile. "They're smart, Bradley. They'll let you lead it, let you do the work, and then they'll break you down. You've got to run smarter than them." A hundred times he repeated it, as **genially** as possible, until Brad burst.

Canter: n. trot or gait, often the three-beat gallop of a horse.
Solitary: adj. alone, solo, without others.
Brood: v. to think about darkly, moodily.
Despondent: adj. emotionally distant and removed, in low spirits.
Annihilate: v. to destroy utterly, obliterate.
Genial: adj. friendly, cheerful, pleasant.

"I gotta lead the whole race!" he shouted. "That's how I run, man!"

"Bradley," said Coach, "if you run my way, I guarantee you'll win."

Brad pulled on a pair of red-white-and-blue Fourth of July socks and ran against Wisconsin's finest. As instructed, he hung back—too far. He was fifteenth at the mile mark, twenty-fourth at the two-mile mark. "What's he doing?" I asked.

"Teaching me a lesson," said Coach **stoically**. Brad made a half-hearted kick, and moved all the way up to twelfth. Then, spent, he dropped back to eighteenth, where he finished. After he crossed the line, he pulled off his jersey, wadded it into a ball, and hurled it into a pine tree. I took it down and pulled off the four safety pins that secured his race number to the jersey. I handed the number and the jersey to his father. I wasn't expecting a laminated copy this time.

Mr. Groff lived **vicariously** through his son—he had never run himself, but came to all the meets and offered us helpful advice, such as "Win, boys!" He was **sanguine** about Brad's finish. "Well he may not have won state," Mr. Groff said, "but he sure did set some records, eh? You boys ever wonder how long they'll last?" As it turned out, those records lasted barely a year.

❄

Brad graduated, leaving behind a team with no hope of success past personal bests. My senior year, on the second day of practice, a wisp of a boy walked into the high school lobby

Stoically: adv. enduring pain and hardship without showing feeling or complaining.
Vicariously: adv. experiencing through the feelings or actions of another person.
Sanguine: adj. cheerfully optimistic.

where we were stretching. "Are you the cross-country team?" he asked. "I looked for you guys for, like, an hour yesterday and I couldn't find you *anywhere!*" He didn't stretch, he just stared **vapidly** into space. This was my introduction to Darnell Perkins, who set his own record immediately: the most directionally impaired runner in the history of cross-country. Fortunately, he was speedy enough to make up for it.

"Whadaya run a mile in?" asked Adam.

"Oh, I don't run the mile," he said. "I've never run cross-country before, either. Mostly I'm an 800-runner. I do a 1:59." You could hear the eyes roll. Didn't run the mile. Didn't run cross. Pushover. Amateur. **Dilettante**. Then, I did the conversions—double and add thirty seconds for a mile, add another thirty seconds and triple it for a 5k and . . . sweet Jesus. Low 15:00s. A minute faster than Brad.

"Are you sure?" I said. "1:59?"

"Oh, no," he said. "Not exactly." I nodded. "It was more like a 1:58.7, or something. I forget."

"Shoot," said Adam. "That ain't nothin'. I run it in 1:05."

"Dude, the world record's, like, 1:40," I said.

"Wait, which one's the 800?" asked Adam.

"Two times around the track," I said.

"No, I run the one-time-around one. What's that called?"

"The 400."

"Oh."

"That's *good!*" said Darnell. "I don't think I could do that."

Darnell's sense of direction proved to be every bit as **acute** as his grasp of distances. The first race that year split the runners

---

Vapid: adj. lacking liveliness; dull.
Dilettante: n. a person with interest in a hobby but no knowledge, commitment or talent.
Acute: adj. having great perception or insight; sharp.

up by grade level, so he ran with the four other freshmen on our team. Most of them were **rookies**—first time on a cross-country course—so Coach briefed them five minutes before the race.

"There's gonna be pushing at the start, so run **assertively**, get clear of the pack, and hook up with your teammates. If you've got to throw an elbow, make sure the officials can't see you. A yellow flag means turn *right*, red means turn *left*, and blue means run straight ahead. When you hit the chute at the end, keep your arms out so no one passes you. And it's hot to-day, so don't hang around the finish line after you're done. It could get kinda pukey." He straightened his sunglasses. "Any questions?"

The freshmen stretched their calves or ran sprints to loosen up. Darnell approached me, looking **perplexed**. "Damn, I didn't understand any of that—it's like red arrows for right and they shoot us at the end?"

I was standing off to one side huddled in my letter jacket. I had the flu. "No there's a *chute*," I said, "like two ribbons on either side that you have to run through."

"They give out ribbons before the end?"

"No. Stop worrying. You won't get lost. Just follow the guy in front of you." So Darnell lined up with our other four guys, the official fired his gun, and two hundred runners were off. Darnell sprinted out to the front of the pack and his teammates followed him.

"One hundred dollars says they fade," said Adam. "Then can we throw them in a lake?"

Rookie: n. a new recruit, usually a first-year member of a sport or team.
Assertive: adj. displaying confidence and self-esteem.
Perplexed: adj. puzzled; baffled over the inability to understand something.

At the half-mile mark, Darnell glided past us, fifteen seconds ahead of the next runner and way ahead of the rest of our guys. "Too fast," said Adam **dubiously**. "He can't hold it."

Darnell was thirty seconds ahead at the halfway mark, when he turned right at a red flag. Fifty spectators started screaming at him. He turned around. With a quarter mile to go, he was fifty seconds ahead. "Sprint for the finish!" Coach yelled. Darnell sprinted like he was riding the shockwave of a nuclear explosion. He **hurtled** toward the finish line and then screeched to a halt when he reached the chute. He eyed it **skeptically**. "Do I just walk through here or what?" he asked a race official, who nodded. So Darnell waved to us, walked the last ten meters of the race and finished a minute ahead of his nearest competitor. 16:40.

"Shoot," said Adam. "I ain't number one no more." He was too distracted to think about the lake.

The sophomores ran, then the juniors, and then it was my turn.

"Tom, if this one is just going to make you sicker, sit it out," Coach said.

"Fine," I gurgled, pointing to the starting line. "I'll be fine. I'll set an example."

Truth be told, I was an ugly runner. I **lumbered**. I once watched video footage of myself running, and I didn't even recognize the runner on the screen: a six-foot-two, hundred-and-fifty-pound guy who waddled and swayed from side to side like a fat man.

My first year, that runner's **gait** had consistently beat only

Dubious: adj. doubting; unsettled in opinion.
Hurtle: v. to move at great speed, usually in a wildly uncontrolled manner.
Skeptical: adj. questioning or doubting, often of accepted opinions.
Lumber: v. moving slowly, heavily and awkwardly.
Gait: n. manner of walking, including pace and step.

one of my teammates: a frail-looking senior nicknamed "Skeeter," short for "Mosquito." He was as thin and fragile as a mosquito, and had a high, buzzing laugh. Years later, I learned that Skeeter had finished a chemotherapy treatment for brain cancer a couple months before I joined the team. So beating the Skeetmeister wasn't exactly something I could boast about.

"The starting line's over there," Coach said. "Over *there*—the one in the middle."

I lined up with the other seniors in the four-foot-wide slot our team had been assigned. The gun went off and I shuffled forward. Every single runner passed me. At the mile mark, I was ahead of two runners out of seventy—one weighed about two hundred and fifty pounds and the other **thrashed** his right arm wildly across his chest with every step he took. When he breathed, he yipped like a dog gnawing on a bone. He stayed right behind me the entire race. "You *got* him, champ!" screamed his coach as we turned the corner for the home stretch. "Take that guy!" The kid **flailed** his way past me to the finish line.

27:40. 69th of 70.

"Sorry, man," said the official at the finish line. "We ran out of ribbons."

❋

Three weeks later I was beaten by Steve Karger, otherwise known as "Sweatpants." Sweatpants was a tiny, googly-eyed guy whose name had been Steve until he wore sweatpants to practice in the middle of August. "My mom was doing the laundry and all my shorts were in there."

Sweatpants was a talker. At practice, on the bus, in the middle

Thrash: v. to hit hard repeatedly.
Flail: v. to wave or swing.

of races, with an audience, or all by himself, he was **loquacious** to no end. We were pretty sure it wasn't mental illness. Rather, he knew it drove some people crazy and loved to see them pop. I didn't really mind until the meet at Nagawaukee Park, which sent out teammates in pairs. Steve and I were supposed to run together in the slow heat.

"What's your goal for today?" asked Coach, as we walked to the line.

"I'm gonna beat Tom! I'm gonna go out there and beat Ace and he's going down and I'm gonna beat him. . . ."

Years before, I had been **christened** Ace. Tom Ace. Like Tomace. Thomas. Not because I was the team's ace, but because someone decided my freshman year that I walked like Jim Carrey in *Ace Ventura: Pet Detective*. It stuck. Kids I didn't even know called me Ace while I walked down the hall at school.

Steve beat me off the line and I lost sight of him. I feared I would suffer the ultimate **indignity** for a captain: to get bumped down to JV. If it had been anyone but Steve, I could have tolerated it—for the sake of the team's betterment. But *Steve*? God, I'd never hear the end of it. I poured on speed and roared past him at the halfway mark. For a moment, I could hear him chanting under his breath, "GottabeatTomgottabeat-TomgottabeatTom . . ." I turned up the speed another notch to get away from the dogged **mantra**.

But the second half of the race was hilly and fatigue crept into my quads. I had spent so much energy trying to catch Steve that I didn't have anything left with which to finish the

Loquacious: adj. talkative.
Christen: v. to be given a name reflective of a quality or characteristic.
Indignity: n. an event that makes a person feel shame.
Mantra: n. a word or motto that embodies a principle; a repeated word or statement.

race. Runners began to re-pass me. Stupid, I thought. My time was going to be **horrendous**—an absolute **travesty**. Steve's fault. Normally I ran a smart race, but Steve had thrown me off. That stupid little elf. As I **shambled** through the last hundred meters, with the crowd packed in on either side, a kid eight inches shorter than me tried to sneak past. It sounded as if he were muttering something under his breath. My name. I stretched out my arm to block him—technically illegal, but commonly done—and the runner backed off.

"Asshole," he rasped, and moved to pass me a second time. I reached out and shoved him hard in the chest, but he stayed on his feet and passed me. However, he was wearing yellow and blue: wrong colors. Not Steve. Seconds later I crossed the line.

"Disqualified—green! Green, number 759, DQ!" A race official pulled me out of line. I was **furious**. I would have been perfectly happy to get disqualified for throwing a punch at Steve, but not at a complete stranger!

"Leave your **pugilism** in the woods, next time," Coach told me, lightly.

"You want me to take that guy out for you?" asked Adam.

"I beat Tom! I beat *Ace*!" Steve shouted. He had. He'd finished two minutes behind me, but he'd beaten me: A disqualified runner is bumped down to last place.

"Shut up, Sweatpants," Adam said, and threw him in the bushes.

❈

Horrendous: adj. very unpleasant or terrible.
Travesty: n. an exaggerated or absurd likeliness or imitation, a parody.
Shamble: v. slow shuffling.
Furious: adj. extremely angry.
Pugilism: n. boxing; the practice of fighting with the fists.

Only one teammate called me by my proper name: sophomore Andy Cera, who was anything but proper. His single goal in life was to score with the "honeys." But every time Andy put the moves on a girl, she was scared off by his enormous **proboscis**. Andy's entire face was built around his nose, an enormous, beak-like structure that might have appeared **aristocratic** on a larger face, but dwarfed all of Andy's other features. When he walked into a room, his nose arrived ten seconds before he did. His failure to find a girlfriend left him feeling **dejected**. "Football players get the honeys. Basketball players get the honeys. But runners—no honeys," he whined.

"Did you ever think you don't have a girlfriend because you call all women 'honeys'?"

He stared back blankly.

"I mean, *I've* got a girlfriend, *Leo* has a girlfriend, *Josh* has a girlfriend, hell, even *Steve* . . ."

"Shut up *Ace*!" he said.

And then one day—one **enchanted**, magical, **supernatural** day—there they were: the honeys. We were running along Menominee River Parkway and in the other direction came the women's team from Divine Savior-Holy Angels, a Catholic girls' high school. Tall girls, short girls, blondes, and brunettes. Girls in T-shirts, sweatshirts, tank tops, and sports bras. "Thank you, God," Andy said.

He slowed way down and smiled. Waved. Punched at the air.

"Like you've never seen girls before?" I said. "I mean, Jesus,

Proboscis: n. the human nose, especially when prominent.
Aristocratic: adj. grand, stylish, and distinguished in manners.
Dejected: adj. sad, depressed, dispirited.
Enchanted: adj. filled with delight and charm, as if cast under a spell.
Supernatural: adj. or n. beyond what is natural; pertaining to a God or deity.

we've got a girls' cross-country team. They ride the bus with us every week."

"That wasn't a girls' team, that was a *women's team*," he said. "I'm going back."

"Don't," I said. "They'll know you're desperate."

"Right," said Andy. "Good, I'll be **subtle**." And as soon as he couldn't see them over his shoulder, he took off faster than I'd ever seen him run, crossed the river at the next bridge, and looped back toward the DSHA team. He was going to overtake them and head them off at the next bridge. The rest of us ran back to school. No sign of Andy.

We stretched and lifted weights. Still nothing. We changed into our street clothes. Nothing. Coach was becoming **agitated** behind his glasses at the thought of Andy wandering among rush hour traffic. An hour later, Andy walked in, face split in half with a grin. He gave us the thumbs up and pounded his chest.

"Did you get lost?" Coach asked.

"Damn, Coach, can we do that run tomorrow? There were *honeys* out there! Hundreds of 'em."

"Like, fifteen," I said.

"Shut up," Andy said. "You don't know nothin'."

It became part of Shayne's Andy imitation, delivered in a **falsetto**: "Ooooh, please, Coach, can't we go on a *honey run*?" Shayne was the token **thespian** of the group. Imitations were a new thing for him; he had gone through a **metamorphosis** over the last two years. When we met in the fourth grade, he

Subtle: adj. quietly delicate; not obvious.
Agitated: adj. nervous, anxious.
Falsetto: n. a very high voice, often used by male singers to sing high notes.
Thespian: n. an actor or actress.
Metamorphosis: n. a complete change or transformation.

spoke to me and three other people. Now he wanted to be a professional actor.

The **catalyst** was our high school's production of *The Music Man*, though I can't claim it was my part as the mayor that inspired him. Shayne came the first night to see me and a couple other friends with bit parts. He returned the second night to watch my eight-year-old brother, who played Winthrop, the **waif** with a speech impediment, who becomes a star flugelhornist.

"He's great," Shayne said.

"Uh, thanks," I said.

"He's the best part. I mean he just gets up there and *sings*. No stage fright. No **apprehension**. Like, nothing." So Shayne, whom I had once recruited to join the cross-country team, went to play tryouts. Our senior year, in *West Side Story*, he played Bernardo—the knife-fighting Puerto Rican gang leader who dances the mambo and gets all the honeys he wants. I played the racist police detective who threatens Bernardo's life. Given that Shayne was **demolishing** my 5k times by two minutes or more, I found it easy to get into character.

However, as **laconic** as Shayne had been when I first met him, he was no match for Phil Dixon, "the silent one." Phil's **taciturnity** was legendary. We knew he was capable of speech—everyone vaguely recalled having heard him say *something*—but no one could recall a specific time. Phil communicated through

Catalyst: n. the person or thing that sets off or causes an event.

Waif: n. a homeless abandoned child.

Apprehension: n. anxiety or fear that something bad or unpleasant will happen.

Demolish: v. to knock down; ruin completely.

Laconic: adj. using few words.

Taciturnity: n. silence; reservation in speaking.

three gestures: the shake, the fast shake, and the nod. There was an **aura** around him that made people ask yes–no questions.

Coach's planning tactics before the sectionals:

"Adam, what's gonna be your time today?"

"Shoot—16:45."

"Tom?"

"17:59."

"Shayne?"

"16:50."

"Phil, are you gonna run a 16:45? [Shake.] 16:50? [Vigorous shake.] 16:40? [Nod.] Great. Darnell?"

"What?"

And so began my final meet. While we were stretching, a tall **reticent** man **materialized** under the oak tree where we had dumped our bags. He appeared out of thin air, like a **chimera**. Sporting a black leather jacket and black pants, he was an **umbrageous**, unsmiling figure. "You looking for Phil?" Coach asked. The man nodded. "Phil!" Coach yelled. Phil turned. A look of total delight transformed his face. He took his hands out of his pockets, straightened his back, and ran to the man and embraced him. The two began speaking, **rapidly, animatedly**, both in voices so quiet and low in **timbre** that we couldn't make out the words.

"Shoot," said Adam. "He *does* talk."

Aura: n. the atmosphere that surrounds a person or thing.
Reticent: adj. keeping ones thoughts, feelings and personal affairs to oneself, restrained.
Materialize: v. to appear, to take physical form.
Chimera: n. an illusion of the imagination.
Umbrageous: adj. spotted with shadows.
Rapidly: adv. quickly, speedily, happening in a short time.
Animated: adj. lively, full of excitement and expression.
Timbre: n. the character of a voice or sound.

I knew nothing about Phil, just that he wanted to go to technical school and that he lived with his grandmother. How did I know even that much? He must have opened his mouth and moved his tongue once, and said, "grandma," and "carpentry."

Phil and the visitor talked **incessantly**, before they finally fell silent and simply stared at one another. Then, Phil walked back to where we were standing stretching with all eyes on him. He **swaggered**. That invisible kid—our No. 2 runner—strutted, smirked, and cracked his knuckles. He made direct eye contact.

"Coach—16:35," said Phil.

❊

It was time. We lined up, all seven of us, two **abreast**, across our box. Darnell and Phil (still smirking) in the front rank, then Adam and Shayne, then Andy and Josh, then me, **unaccompanied**.

Josh turned to me. "I got 'em in my bag. Soon as I'm done. A whole pack."

Josh was our in-house chimney. He loved to smoke.

"But none this week, right?" I asked.

"None," said Josh. "Well, four. Four yesterday. And one this morning. And when I'm done."

I frowned.

"Chill out, Ace, it's not like I count anyway."

I wanted to scream at him that clearly he *did* count, but we'd had the conversation a million times. He never listened.

Incessant: adj. constant, continuing without pause or interruption.
Swagger: v. to walk or behave with an arrogant confidence.
Abreast: adv. alongside, side-by-side.
Unaccompanied: adj. without a companion, escort, or partner; alone.

As the No. 6 man, Josh counted in the event of a tie. More importantly, if one of our front-runners was injured or had a bad day, his score counted instead of theirs.

At sectionals two years before, at this very same course, I had been the No. 6. The course was a hard one and I had known I didn't have a good shot at a personal-best time, so I dogged it, safe in the knowledge that I didn't count. Then, with a half mile to go, I passed our No. 5, limping off to one side of the course, and suddenly I *did* count. Our front four had run blazing times and then sat for five minutes before I crossed the finish line. Had I run full out, we would have qualified for state.

But there wasn't time to recount this to Josh yet again before the start of the race. The gun went off, I stumbled out of the box and was forced to the back of the pack. I peeked over my shoulder to see how many people I was ahead of. None. I laughed. Then, I put my head down and ran, calm and controlled, and passed people in droves.

Just short of mile two, I found Josh, pulled off to one side wheezing. "I can't breathe," he said.

I grabbed him by the jersey and threw him back onto the course. He stopped again, but I hung onto the shoulder strap of his singlet and dragged him behind me. It was **savage**; I had no sympathy for that smoker. I was mostly worried about ripping off his singlet—the **gossamer**, sleeveless uniform tops we all wore—and allowing him to escape. In Josh's case it would have been easy. In a **characteristic** fit of **machismo**, he had asked for an extra-large when uniforms were handed out, but

Savage: adj. fierce, violent and uncontrolled.
Gossamer: adj. light, delicate, or insubstantial.
Characteristic: adj. typical of a person, place or thing.
Machismo: n. strong or aggressive masculine pride or behavior.

the top was so big and Josh was so **emaciated** that it slid right off. He'd bound the straps with athletic tape to keep it on.

Josh stumbled a few steps behind me, then collected himself and zipped past me. I was worried. If Josh were back with me, we'd never win a tie-breaker. Then I hit the second mile at 11:20 and realized that Josh wasn't back with me, I was up with Josh. The last half mile contained a steep, **precipitous** ascent, followed by a sharp, **circuitous** downhill, where the path narrowed to single file. There was jockeying ahead of me—someone moved off the track, into the woods, walking parallel with the course. Josh.

"Kleep RONGING!" I garbled my command through exhaustion and pulled him onto the path behind me. It was **anathema** to touch another runner and I didn't want to be DQ-ed again. But we were still in the woods and no one was watching. Josh followed me down the hill, and then we emerged from the forest into an open grassy clearing, the last quarter mile. Josh saw the crowd that lined both sides of the trail leading up to the finish line and took off. I **labored** to keep up with him, but he pulled away and finished 50 yards ahead of me.

17:44! I was **elated**! I'd spent the past four years trying to break 18:00. Our front five had all finished under 17:00—personal records all around, which almost certainly meant we had qualified for state. We started whooping it up.

All of us, that is, except for Darnell. He was standing next

Emaciated: adj. extremely thin or weak, usually because of illness or lack of food.

Precipitous: adj. dangerously high or steep; sudden, without thought or warning.

Circuitous: adj. indirect, longer than the most direct route.

Anathema: n. something or someone intensely disliked; a formal ban.

Labor: v. to work hard, particularly physical effort.

Elated: adj. filled with extreme happiness and pride.

to Coach, smiling **vacuously**. Coach Blaha, normally **serene** even in the face of disaster, looked **apoplectic**.

"Where was your kick?" he asked Darnell. "You were in eighth and you could have taken both of those guys in front of you!"

"I don't like passing people at the end," said Darnell. "Besides, I still go to state."

"NOOOOO!" howled Coach. "It's the top *seven*. The top *seven* individual runners go to state."

"Really?" said Darnell. "I thought it was the top ten." He shrugged. "I got three more years." Darnell joined the rest of us as we danced around. We'd qualified as a team, in second place. State qualifiers! Five guys under seventeen minutes—it was impossible *not* to qualify with performances like that. A huge, **unambiguous** victory. We hoisted some of the girls onto our shoulders and paraded around. A patch for our letter jackets: STATE QUALIFIER.

We gathered around Coach to hear the official results. He was standing **rigidly**.

"I am . . . I'm . . . you guys. I am so proud of you guys," he said.

It dawned on me. "We didn't make it," I said.

"Last three years, it would have been enough. Last three years. I am so proud of you guys. Fourth place, I think." Then he stopped speaking. The announcer worked his way up from fifteenth place. We were tied for fifth.

"That's wrong," Coach snarled. "They're wrong. You can't tie. Our sixth man beat theirs. We won fifth alone." He stood,

Vacuous: adj. mindless, empty, showing lack of content.
Serene: adj. calm, peaceful, tranquil.
Apoplectic: adj. extremely angry, furious.
Unambiguous: adj. clear, with no uncertainty.
Rigid: adj. stiff, unmoving.

trembling, for a moment longer, then took off his sunglasses and wiped his eyes.

"Dude, Coach," said Josh. "Now we know why you wear sunglasses, right?"

"One reason among others," Coach said.

"Shut up, Josh," said Andy. He patted Coach on the back. "You need a hankie or something, man?"

We bought a long-sleeve T-shirt for Coach and signed it across the back, with messages from each of us. Phil just signed his name. I stenciled the words MISSION ACCOMPLISHED across the top, a reference to the phrase "On a Mission," which Coach had put on our T-shirts. He'd designed them himself—a picture of a runner **superimposed** over the state of Wisconsin, with a crosshair centered on Wisconsin Rapids, where the state meet was held. We were psyched about "On a Mission" as a **mantra**, until our first meet, when **random** runners and spectators kept yelling at us, "On a mission from *God*," using funny accents, during our warm-ups.

"I think people are **mocking** the shirts," I said.

"No, that's from *The Blues Brothers*," Coach said. None of us had seen it. "You're kidding. It's an awesome flick. Great quote."

"Coach," said Andy. "One word: lame."

I brought the T-shirt to our awards dinner, wrapped in a box. Everyone got gag gifts—my disqualification earned me the "Cheater, Cheater, Pumpkin Eater Award" for "**egregious**

Superimpose: v. to place something over something else, usually so that both are still visible.

Mantra: n. a word or motto that embodies a principle; a repeated word or statement.

Random: adj. arbitrary, assorted by chance.

Mock: v. to tease or laugh at, to ridicule or imitate laughably.

Egregious: adj. outrageously bad.

and **felonious** behavior **unbecoming** of a captain." Apparently they didn't remember Brad. Then came the two real awards. Most Valuable Runner went to Darnell, who looked pleased and surprised.

Coach continued. "You might say our Most Improved Runner dropped ten minutes over the course of the season," he said.

I turned red.

"I dropped ten minutes?" said Darnell. "Wow. That's a lot!"

"No," said Coach. "Tom did." So I got a parallelogram-shaped patch to sew on my letter jacket after all.

"There's one more gift I wanted to give out tonight," said Coach. "And that was T-shirts that said MISSION ACCOMPLISHED. Except, we didn't qualify for state. So maybe next year."

Aghast, I took the T-shirt out and handed it to him. "Umm, we thought it was mission accomplished since everybody had personal best times. . . . Jeez, I'm sorry, that's pretty **asinine**. . . . I mean I guess we didn't . . ."

"Shut up," Coach said. "It's perfect." He laid it out on a desk and smoothed the wrinkles from the fabric. "Perfect." Then, he leaned in close to read the **inscriptions**, removed his sunglasses from his pocket and slipped them on.

✳ **Tom Miller** grew up in Wauwatosa, Wisconsin. On his first date, his girlfriend accidentally left him behind at the Olive Garden. He majored in English at Harvard and earned a master of fine arts in creative writing from Notre Dame. He's a five-time marathon finisher.

Felonious: adj. relating to crime or felony.
Unbecoming: adj. not attractive, fitting or appropriate.
Aghast: adj. filled with horror or shock.
Asinine: adj. extremely stupid or foolish.
Inscription: n. words or symbols written or carved into something, such as a book or monument.

CONFESSIONS OF AN INSANE INTERN

Kara Loewentheil

Volunteers always get the easy jobs, right? That's what I assumed when the nurses at the psychiatric hospital asked me to take the patients on a cigarette break. I had been volunteering at the hospital for long enough to know the residents' simple smoking routine. If they followed directions, **participated** in therapy, and took their meds, they were allowed to step outside for a quick puff every few hours. All I had to do was lead this short **expedition** to the hospital's outdoor courtyard. And to make this **vigilance** even easier, the courtyard was **circumscribed** by a ten-foot-high wooden fence. No one could wander off if they tried. Or so I thought.

Because on the lucky day I was sent outside, one of my patients proved that this fence was not as **insurmountable** as it seemed. I was busy keeping track of our **motley** group, which included everyone from a twenty-year-old anorexic to an eighty-five-year-old-man who was convinced that

Participate: v. to take part in something.
Expedition: n. an excursion made by a group for a specific purpose.
Vigilance: n. being alert and aware.
Circumscribe: v. to limit; bound; restrain within a boundary.
Insurmountable: adj. impossible to overcome.
Motley: adj. composed of diverse or discordant parts; a random assemblage.

then-President Clinton was sending him messages through the television. Most were milling about, **voraciously** devouring their cigarettes, while a few lay **supine** on the grass, staring up at the clouds. Meanwhile Seymour, a male patient on the ward, was **executing** his escape plan behind me. When I turned around, I caught sight of him scaling the hospital's wooden fence in his slippers.

"Seymour!" I exclaimed, my mouth **agape**. When he reached the top, Seymour briefly straddled the fence, and then his slippers disappeared over the other side. He was gone. Something told me volunteers weren't supposed to return from cigarette break with fewer residents than they had taken out. I had no idea how to escape this **quandary**. So I froze.

❉

While my friends were hiking the Appalachian Trail or apprenticing with carpenters for *their* senior projects, I had signed up to be a **vassal** at a psychiatric hospital. So here I was, spending eight hours a day in a locked ward, where shoelaces were **confiscated** and (as I had most recently learned) people scaled ten-foot fences in their laceless, slip-on shoes.

I had **naively** chosen mental health because I was **inherently** good at talking to strangers. People seemed to find me

Voracious: adj. having a huge appetite; extremely eager.
Supine: adj. lying on the back.
Execute: v. to do, perform, carry out.
Agape: adj. with the mouth wide open.
Quandary: n. a dilemma; a state of uncertainty about what to do.
Vassal: n. a slave; a subservient or subordinate person.
Confiscate: v. to take away especially by authority.
Naive: adj. unsophisticated; simplistic; unexposed to the world.
Inherent: adj. belonging intrinsically; innate.

accessible, sharing intimate details of their lives for no apparent reason. When I was only twelve, a man approached me at a local strip mall to share that he was better endowed than Cal Ripkin, the Baltimore baseball **legend**. The man then offered to sell me baseball cards he had stapled to a boogie board (which I nearly bought as a **souvenir** of the bizarre experience). In drugstores, little old ladies would come up to me and ask me what kind of pantyhose they should buy. Once, while I was on a field trip to the Baltimore Harbor with my writing class, a middle-aged woman sat down beside me on a bench on the waterfront and **divulged** her daughter's suicide in **heartrending** detail. Then she simply got up and left, leaving her tragic **visage** imprinted on my memory. I never forgot the **dolorous** story.

People in my high school treated me like a confessional, too. I was always the first to know when one girl hooked up with another's boyfriend, or someone's mom busted them with a bottle of beer. These confessions were so **abundant** that I took them as a sign. I was destined to become a psychologist. The profession struck me as **cerebral**, requiring some real smarts, but I thought it also required an **empathetic** nature, so it would utilize my **innate** talent. If you left

Accessible: adj. reachable; easy to communicate or deal with.
Legend: 1. a person or thing who is well-known or famous in popular myth; 2. a story from the past.
Souvenir: n. a token of remembrance.
Divulge: v. to tell or make known previously secret information.
Heartrending: adj. causing extreme grief, pity, or heartache.
Visage: n. the face; the countenance, or look of a person.
Dolorous: adj. mournful; expressing or causing sorrow or pain.
Abundant: adj. plentiful; present in great quantity.
Cerebral: adj. pertaining to the cerebrum or brain; intellectual.
Empathetic: adj. understanding and being sensitive to the feelings and experiences of others.
Innate: adj. existing in one from birth; inborn.

the decision to me, I would have skipped medical school altogether and gone straight to being a psychologist.

That's why the **notion** of volunteering at a psychiatric hospital appealed to me so much. On the first day of my project, I arrived oozing **felicity** and confidence. The hospital was set on beautiful landscaped hills and had the air of a **magnificent** European chalet. Unlike public hospitals, this one was private, so it could afford to maintain this **aesthetic**.

The inside of the hospital, however, didn't look as **genteel**. In fact, the psych ward had more in common with a high school than I expected. Not long after they buzzed me through the high-security front door of the hospital, I began imagining connections between the **trivial** high school world I knew so well, and the more tragic **microcosm** of the psych ward that I was just getting to know.

I soon discovered that mental hospitals have their own version of cheerleaders. These women were generally blonde and **garrulous** and never seemed to have actual diagnoses. We all just **tacitly** understood that they were a bit too sensitive for **quotidian domestic** life. Their husbands and **fawning**

Notion: n. a general idea; a somewhat vague belief.

Felicity: n. happiness; a source of happiness.

Magnificent: adj. great in size or extent; splendid; brilliant.

Aesthetic: n. pertaining to beauty.

Genteel: adj. elegantly graceful; having an upper-class or aristocratic manner or appearance.

Trivial: adj. of little importance or significance; minor; unimportant.

Microcosm: n. a little world; a small part representative of a bigger world.

Garrulous: adj. excessively talkative, especially on trivial matters.

Tacit: adj. understood or implied without being stated; implied but not expressed.

Quotidian: adj. daily; usual.

Domestic: adj. relating to the household.

Fawn: v. to give exaggerated flattery or affection.

boyfriends visited often, bringing them silk pajamas to wear around the common room.

The counterparts of these cheerleaders were the midlife-crisis men—or, in high school terms, the jocks. Former advertising executives or corporate lawyers, these men were generally good looking. Like the **fragile** women, they never seemed to have a specific medical problem, though the nurses assured me they were coming out of major breakdowns. They wandered around the ward looking apologetic and **sedate**.

Any **racy** romance that might have gone on between the jocks and the cheerleaders was cut short by hospital policy. The ward did not allow private contact. These rules sounded uncannily familiar to me, as I came from a household where doors remained open when visitors of the opposite sex entered my siblings' rooms. The psych ward had an even more **draconian** rule. They also prohibited all **reclining**. Yes, one foot had to be on the floor during waking hours. When the patients complained about this rule, they sounded almost like **indignant** teenagers.

Next on the totem pole of the psych ward were the too-cool-for-school types. These patients had been hospitalized a few times before and knew the routine. Like the creative kids and the "goth" group at any high school, these patients were generally artistic and emotional types. They spent most of their time **deigning** to make art in the crafts room or **fervently** arguing over who smoked the finest cigarettes.

Fragile: adj. easily broken; delicate; brittle.

Sedate: adj. even-tempered; quiet and steady.

Racy: adj. lively, entertaining, and mildly sexually exciting.

Draconian: adj. harshly repressive; severe. (Origin: Draco, the writer of harsh ancient Greek Laws.)

Recline: v. to lean back.

Indignant: adj. feeling or showing anger, esp. righteous anger; resentful.

Deign: v. to stoop or do something one feels is below one's dignity.

Fervent: adj. with passion and intensity.

Finally, there were the loners. Sadly, the lives of these patients were **dominated** by the **caprices** of their brain chemistry. They were the **listless** types, the severely depressed, the **delirious**, those who were unhinged even when heavily medicated. Their **erratic** moods changed day by day. In high school, they would have doodled **anarchy** symbols in their notebooks and managed to go four years without uttering a word in class.

The one activity that connected all of these **incompatible** groups was crossword puzzles. Crosswords are the **unifying** factor of the mentally ill. With the exception of smoking, nothing was as popular. Walking around our ward's lounge, you would have thought that mental illnesses were **curable** through crosswords. We did an incredible number of puzzles, particularly on the days the ward was **quiescent** due to the weather.

When not filling in crosswords with pencils, I was having fun with the DSM IV, otherwise known as the *Diagnostic and Statistical Manual*, or "the standard psychiatric diagnostic tool." I used it to **theorize** about what was wrong with all my family members and friends. You'd be surprised how **pleasurable** this game can be. For example, without the psych-ward bible, I never would have guessed that my neighbor's son had

---

Dominate: v. to govern; control; hold control.
Caprice: n. a whim; a sudden, impulsive action or notion.
Listless: adj. lacking energy or enthusiasm.
Delirious: adj. raving and confused.
Erratic: adj. wandering; off course; lacking consistency.
Anarchy: n. lack of government; a state of lawlessness.
Incompatible: unable to be used together; not harmonious.
Unify: v. to make into a single whole.
Curable: adj. able to be remedied or corrected.
Quiescent: adj. inactive, latent, and dormant.
Theorize: v. to form a theory about.
Pleasurable: adj. pleasant; gratifying.

oppositional-defiant disorder. Before, I'd just considered him **odious**. The DSM game could get trickier, though, especially when you started skimming with yourself in mind. One particularly dramatic day, I became convinced I had borderline personality disorder. Soon, however, I tempered the self-diagnosis. By the next morning, I was "indecisive."

❖

Indecision might be preferable to mental illness, but my indecision sure didn't help when Seymour scaled the hospital fence. Should I climb after him, leaving everyone on smoke break behind? Would this spark an **abrupt** flood of **opportunists** and turn my mistake into total **fiasco**? Or should I herd everyone back inside and beg for backup? What was the less **pitiful** way for a young volunteer to respond? In which direction should I flee?

I never actually made a decision to cry; it just sort of happened. Tears streamed down my face as I ran inside in search of help. A nurse? Doctor? Anyone with the **jurisdiction** to fix this mess?! I prepared myself for the staff's **remonstrance**, certain I deserved it. I might have volunteered at the psychiatric hospital with **altruistic** intentions, but I had screwed up in a big, bad way.

Odious: adj. hateful; repugnant.
Indecision: n. irresolution; lack of decision; wavering.
Abrupt: adj. sudden and unexpected.
Opportunist: n. one who is quick to grasp opportunities.
Fiasco: n. total failure.
Pitiful: adj. deserving pity and sympathy.
Jurisdiction: n. the power to make and enforce laws.
Remonstrance: n. an objection; protest.
Altruistic: adj. unselfish regard for or devotion to the welfare of others.

My wet face must have been a pitiful sight, because the nurses and staff reacted with alarm. They rushed over to ask what happened.

"I . . ." I pointed toward the courtyard, barely able to **articulate** a word. "Seymour . . ."

The charge nurse gave me a **puzzled** look.

"It happened so fast . . ."

I finally gulped my way through the **narrative**: One of the patients was gone and the rest were now alone in the courtyard. And yes, this had all **transpired** in under three minutes.

I was sure they would fire me on the spot. In fact, I offered my resignation before my tears had even dried. More than **humiliated**, I felt **wretched**. But the ward nurse just laughed at my confession. Apparently, this incident was not only **comical**, but routine.

"Don't be ridiculous," she said with total **equanimity**. "This happens all the time."

Trying hard to believe that patients really did turn into fugitives on a regular basis, I went to the bathroom and splashed cold water on my face. But no matter how much I splashed, the feeling of **incompetence** wouldn't **abate**.

I came back the next day, and the next, and the next. I

Articulate: v. to say or speak distinctly, with clear separation of syllables.

Puzzled: adj. perplexed; confused.

Narrative: n. a story.

Transpire: v. to happen; occur.

Humiliate: v. to subject to shame or disgrace; mortify.

Wretched: adj. deeply distressed in body and mind; dejected.

Comical: adj. funny; humorous.

Equanimity: n. evenness of mind or temper; calmness under stress.

Incompetence: n. the lack of the necessary skills; the state of being unqualified.

Abate: v. to diminish; lessen.

persevered through my senior project at the psych ward, though for its remainder, I had an **ominious** suspicion that the patients were all laughing at me—the **inept** teenage helper. When we sat down to do crosswords, I wondered if they were just **patronizing** *me* with the game. I seemed to have developed my very own case of obsessive paranoia.

To my relief, Seymour did come back. In fact, by the time his parents brought our **maverick** patient back to the ward, the rest of his wardmates were thankfully **engrossed** in something else. And this time, it was even more exciting than crossword puzzles. Their newfound **devilry**: prank-calling local businesses.

It took Seymour a while to earn his smoke-break privileges back. He **vindicated** himself with a couple of weeks of good behavior and quiet crossword puzzles. When he did rejoin the cigarette clan, I took a much more **defensive** approach to my smoke-break duties. Under my watch, Seymour had to remain on the steps instead of the grass—yes, two feet, at all times. If worse came to worst, I figured, I could at least tackle him before he reached the fence. My senior project may not have been **edifying** in the way I had hopesd, but it did teach me a thing or two about being **decisive**.

Persevere: v. to persist in something.

Ominous: adj. foretelling disaster; threatening.

Inept: adj. not apt, fit, or suited.

Patronize: v. to treat with condescension.

Maverick: n. a nonconformist; an independent person who does not go along with the group.

Engross: v. to fully occupy.

Devilry: n. malicious mischief; wickedness.

Vindicate: v. to free from accusation or blame.

Defensive: adj. protective; supportive in the face of criticism.

Edify: v. to instruct and improve, especially in moral and religious knowledge.

Decisive: adj. final; conclusive; resolute.

❊ **Kara Loewentheil** grew up in Baltimore, Maryland, where "Hon" is a proper noun, and attended Yale University. She managed to get a degree by writing stories and starting her thesis the morning it was due. She is currently studying at Harvard Law School, focusing on women's issues. Although she has not been back to a psychiatric hospital since her internship, Kara does visit her family on the holidays and tends to refer to them as "the inmates."

8

CONFESSIONS OF A GHETTO SOCCER STAR

Lauren Keane

A muscular leg was pinning my head against the truck window, and I didn't know whose it was. My soccer team made a habit of traveling this way: in a three-layer pile of athletes, all **compressed** into a single Chevy Suburban. It wasn't exactly cozy, but it was our style.

On spring afternoons, all eighteen of us zoomed down the freeway in our Chevy, leaving the city of San Francisco behind. Our destination was suburbia, where we would face down **formidable** athletes from private schools—girls who'd been kicking around soccer balls since they learned to walk. The jam-packed ride was our opportunity to **devise** a battle plan, to pretend we had a shot at winning. But as numbness crept up our tangled limbs, the conversation usually **degenerated**—from talking smack about our enemy team, to talking smack about each other.

"Will you get your *butt* off my *leg*, yo? It's been asleep for, like, a half hour now."

"How 'bout you get yours off my face."

"Yo, *move over*. I can't feel my . . ."

Compress: v. to pack tightly together, condense.
Formidable: adj. causing fear or apprehension; having qualities that discourage approach.
Devise: v. to think out; concoct; scheme.
Degenerate: v. to deteriorate; sink into an inferior state.

126

Just as we were about to drop kick one another, we'd pull up to our **opponents'** school: a **manicured** suburban campus with the **aesthetic** of a country club. All eighteen of us tumbled out of the truck at once, the way people in Volkswagen bug commercials do. Our Chevy was missing three hubcaps and **desperately** needed a bath. Anamaria, who crawled out first, wrote WASH ME! on the rear window with her pinkie finger.

Our team would have numbered only seventeen, but Ngoc, our ninety-four-pound runt, had **protested** loudly and squeezed her way into the van. She was a **miniature** terror on the field, weaving between defenders with **preternatural** speed. But what she did even better was put her **mighty** lungs and colorful vocabulary to good use at games against prep schools. She became the **mascot** of the Lowell High School girls' soccer team—as scrappy as the rest of us city girls, and even more **vociferous**.

Ngoc leapt from the back of the truck and sped off toward the field with an **exuberant** grin on her face.

"GRASS!" she cried **reverently**, falling to her knees. Ngoc ran her hand along the three-inch high emerald carpet, which

Opponent: n. an adversary.
Manicure: v. to trim; polish; groom.
Aesthetic: n. a particular theory or conception of beauty or art; a taste or approach to what is pleasing to the senses and eye.
Desperate: adj. having lost hope; suffering extreme need or anxiety.
Protest: v. to object or indicate disapproval.
Miniature: n. something small of its kind.
Preternatural: adj. extraordinary; beyond what is natural.
Mighty: adj. powerful.
Mascot: n. an animal or person symbolizing a group.
Vociferous: adj. exclaiming; clamorous; noisy.
Exuberant: adj. effusive in feeling or expression.
Reverently: adj. with awe and respect; worshipping.

looked **iridescent** in the afternoon sun. She **nuzzled** her cheek against the **velvety** turf, then sat up and **swiveled** around to flash us a **mischievous** grin.

We were used to Ngoc's **antics**. She wouldn't drive a half hour in a cramped van without cracking a joke upon arrival. **Decorum** was the least of Ngoc's concerns.

"Suburbs," Anamaria practically spit as she **surveyed** the silent row of **palatial** houses across the street. She **hefted** her backpack higher onto her shoulders, leaning forward to balance the weight. "How does *anyone* live here?"

"I guess if you're boring, you don't mind living in a boring place," suggested Jen, our **quiet** captain. Jen had a fireball left-foot shot. Her dad was the one who loaned us the Chevy on game days, knowing that our school district couldn't even afford to bus us to school, much less **transport** us to away games.

A few soccer balls rolled out of his rusty **behemoth** and bounced off into the parking lot. A particularly **grimy** one hit the side of an ivory Mercedes parked nearby, sending its alarm

Iridescent: adj. glittering with changeable colors, like a rainbow.
Nuzzle: v. to nestle; snuggle.
Velvety: adj. something of similar texture to a fabric with a thick, soft pile.
Swivel: v. to pivot; spin around.
Mischievous: adj. maliciously or playfully; annoying.
Antic: n. attention-drawing behavior.
Decorum: n. propriety.
Survey: v. view; scrutinize.
Palatial: adj. grand, like a palace.
Heft: v. to heave; hoist.
Quiet: adj. composed, subdued, not loud.
Transport: v. carry from one place to another.
Behemoth: n. a huge, powerful person or animal.
Grimy: adj. dirty.

system into **shriek** mode. Chris, our goalkeeper, **trotted** over to **reclaim** the **wayward** soccer ball—which was now firmly wedged under the shiny car.

Chris hailed from the Philippines and, unlike most of our slender opponents, she was no **waif**. While Chris wriggled around on the asphalt to retrieve our ball, our opponents appeared.

Dressed in ironed uniforms, the girls marched through the parking lot toward the field in a neat, double-file line. As they passed Chris, their procession bottlenecked and a few of them slowed down to **deride** the girl lying on the pavement like a car mechanic. Our **adversaries** all had **identical** black Adidas gym bags and carried them perfectly **parallel** to the ground. They wore crisp **azure** uniform jerseys tucked into their black shorts. When they reached the field, the **prim** ladies lined up their athletic **regalia** on the sidelines and **proceeded** straight into a warm-up lap.

Anamaria and I joined Ngoc on the field and glared at the enemy as they trotted toward us.

"Oh God, not the hair-ribbon thing," Anamaria muttered.

Shriek: n. shrill outcry or utterance.
Trot: v. to go at a brisk pace between a walk and a run.
Reclaim: v. to regain possession of.
Wayward: adj. turning or changing irregularly.
Waif: n. a stray animal or person.
Deride: v. laugh at contemptuously; mock.
Adversaries: n. opponents in a contest; enemy.
Identical: adj. the same.
Parallel: adj. of lines or planes, never intersecting, equidistant at all points.
Azure: adj. and n. sky blue.
Prim: adj. stiffly formal.
Regalia: n. emblems, insignia.
Proceed: v. go forward; continue or renew progress.

Indeed: We counted nine ponytails **bobbing** left to right, tied with blue and white ribbons.

"What is this, cheerleader camp?" Anamaria added, in her usual **caustic** way.

Chris, having finally **retrieved** the ball, came jogging over to us. I could tell she was trying not to look upset, but the enemy's giggles had clearly **discomfited** her.

"OK, Keanie," she said to me, shoving the ball a bit too **brusquely** into my lap. "That's it. Now you *really* gotta take her out."

I had no clue which "she" Chris was talking about. Had my team already pinpointed a player for me to **annihilate**?

"Yeah," Chris continued. "Just do one of your I'm-chasing-you-down-the-sideline-oh-crap!-you-fell-over! numbers."

The gang voiced their **approbation**, while tugging on socks and shin guards.

"Dude, I bet those prep-school freaks'll beat Keanie silly if she does."

"Don't worry. We gotcha, Keanie. Those anorexic chicks won't know what hit 'em."

"Yeah, girl, just stare her down like the last game."

There was nothing my teammates enjoyed more than talking smack. I had knocked over one of these suburban girls in a previous game and my **aggression** had become team **lore**. But

---

Bob: v. to move jerkily; go up and down quickly.
Caustic: adj. severely critical or sarcastic; corrosive.
Retrieve: v. to find again; recover; regain.
Discomfit: v. to embarrass; frustrate; disconcert.
Brusquely: adv. abruptly; curtly.
Annihilate: v. destroy utterly; reduce to nothing.
Approbation: n. approval, commendation.
Aggression: v. an act of hostility; an assault or encroachment.
Lore: n. the knowledge about a particular subject.

truthfully, my **infamous** "slide-tackle" was a **mishap**. I was chasing down an opponent when I stumbled and shot out my left leg, mistakenly tripping her up. As I recovered the ball, she **limped** off the field with a **fractured** ankle, **seething** with anger.

But my teammates didn't know the accidental part of this story. They expected me to target any **meddlesome** girl who dared curse, throw an elbow, look at us funny, or score. As I laced up my cleats and listened to their pregame **rhetoric**, I couldn't bring myself to divulge the truth: I had no clue how to slide-tackle. All I'd aimed to do was fall on my butt instead of my face.

Thankfully, there was a natural **transition** in our conversation.

"Hey guys, the 'Busch is here," one of the girls said, prompting us all to glance up.

Ernie Feibusch, our **septuagenarian** coach, had just rolled through the prep school's wrought-iron gates. He drove an old Cadillac, which was so long it took up a space and a half of parking. Between his clunker and our "team van," the prep school lot wasn't looking so **pristine** anymore.

Our coach **emerged** from the driver's seat, clutching a

Infamous: adj. publicly known for an evil reputation or act; famous for negative reasons.

Mishap: n. an unfortunate occurrence.

Limp: v. to walk favoring one leg; go unsteadily.

Fracture: n. a breaking, especially of a bone.

Seethe: v. to be agitated; suffer violent internal excitement.

Meddlesome: adj. disposed to interfering with what is not one's concern.

Rhetoric: n. unnecessarily exaggerated or insincere speech or language; bombast.

Transition: n. change from one place or state to another.

Septuagenarian: n. a person between seventy and eighty years old.

Pristine: adj. original; unspoiled; fresh and clean as if new.

Emerge: v. to come forth from something that conceals.

clipboard in one hand and a **dilapidated** soccer ball in the other. He squinted and glanced over at us. **Splayed** in a pile of hefty backpacks, my teammates were anything but organized. In **lieu** of brand-name athletic gear, we brought our cleats in pink plastic Chinatown grocery bags. But he didn't seem to mind our **haphazard** appearance. Our coach **summoned** his usual burst of energy and drop-kicked the ball across the lot toward us.

"The 'Busch" was the **sole** reason most of us could play soccer. A **devout** coach, he had convinced our **impecunious** school district to fund a girls' soccer team. Most of our girls were complete **neophytes** on the soccer field, so his job was not an easy one. Lucky for us, Feibusch was a veteran coach. He had spent forty years pacing the sidelines of San Francisco soccer fields with his hands behind his back and his head tucked down to his chin. Our old coach's game-time posture seemed to **accentuate** the slump in his spine. If our field had had grass, Feibusch would have **abraded** it with his back-and-forth movements.

But grass wasn't in the budget at Lowell. We learned to dribble a soccer ball on a dirt lot, guiding the ball through a minefield of gopher holes and gravel patches. The 'Busch was **undeterred** by the sorry state of our field. Instead, he declared

---

Dilapidated: adj. ruined, or fallen into partial or total ruin.

Splayed: adj. spread out; turned outward; awkward.

Lieu: n. place.

Haphazard: adj. occurring by chance; accidental; random.

Summon: v. to rouse; call or send for, with authority.

Sole: adj. unique; only; alone.

Devout: adj. devoted to, especially religion or religious worship.

Impecunious: adj. without money; poor.

Neophyte: n. a beginner; a novice.

Accentuate: v. to stress; emphasize.

Abrade: v. to wear away by friction; roughen by rubbing.

Undeterred: adj. not discouraged or stopped.

"Field Appreciation Days," which were his **sarcastic** version of turf **maintenance**. We'd arrive at practice ready to play soccer, only to hear him order us to "grab a shovel." For the next hour, we'd push dirt around our field, filling its most **treacherous** holes.

For someone over seventy, the 'Busch was quite **robust**. He liked to show off his quads by wearing a pair of ultra-short light blue soccer shorts. His red ears **protruded**, especially with his faded Lowell cap resting on them. Feibusch had over-grown bushy gray eyebrows, which seemed to move around more than his lips. Whether he was laughing or cursing, his eyes sparkled just the same. And our coach certainly did his share of swearing, armed with a mouthful of **coarse** language straight out of his WWII days—an **unpredictable** mix of German, English, and God knows what else.

"Ya SLICED it!" he'd bellow at us from midfield when we spun the ball off to the side. "What the hell were you THINK-ING?!"

He ranted. He hollered. He got almost as many yellow-card fouls as we did. Some people at Lowell were skeptical of his "**eccentric** coaching style" and wrote articles in the school paper **challenging** it. But for every letter of complaint sent to the school principal, one of his players would write two in support

Sarcastic: adj. being or using sarcasm; using sharp sartorial wit.
Maintenance: n. the act of up keeping and preserving equipment or property.
Treacherous: adj. unreliable; likely to betray trust.
Robust: adj. strong; vigorous.
Protrude: v. to stick out; project.
Coarse: adj. crude; unrefined.
Unpredictable: adj. unable to foretell; unexpected.
Eccentric: adj. deviating from the usual or recognized form; unconventional.
Challenge: v. to dispute as being unjust, invalid, or outmoded; confront.

of him. We **tolerated** him and his strange, **authoritarian** style for a simple reason: He was a great coach.

After all, the 'Busch had trained us well enough to **recapture** the city championship year after year—though these steady victories said less about the **merit** of our team and more about the **paucity** of our competition in San Francisco proper. We easily **trounced** most of the public schools in our league. Just when Feibusch thought these victories were going to our heads, he would schedule games outside of the city, where suburban teams gave us rude awakenings. According to Feibusch, an occasional defeat was **salutary** for even the best athletes.

Though we lost by double digits at away games, we weren't hopeless. Every now and then, we'd actually win. Today's ponytailed team had just narrowly squeaked by us last year. All of us **lamented** this loss and tried to **attribute** it to luck. Sure, they were solid athletes, but these suburban girls were more about show than skill. We were determined to come back with a **vengeance** this time. The only thing worse than losing to **ostentatious** suburb girls was losing to them twice. Or as the 'Busch would put it more **succinctly**: "I don't care if it's pretty, just put the damn ball in the damn net!"

Tolerate: v. to bear with patience; to endure without complaint or ill effect.
Authoritarian: adj. ruling by absolute authority.
Recapture: v. to take again; recover.
Merit: n. a commendable quality; worthiness; character or conduct deserving reward.
Paucity: n. smallness of quantity or number.
Trounce: v. defeat divisively; thrash.
Salutary: adj. beneficial; caring.
Lament: v. to express sorrow.
Attribute: v. to consider something as resulted by a cause; ascribe.
Vengeance: n. retributive punishment; revenge.
Ostentatious: adj. a pretentious display.
Succinct: adj. concise; brief.

When the whistle blew, the eighteen of us huddled at the edge of the field. Chris knelt in the center, seventeen hands stacked on top of her head in a sloppy pile.

"All right ladies," she began, "let's show these rich kids what it's like to play *without* three layers of mascara on."

We **mustered** our **guttural** ghetto voices and sounded the war cry: "LOWELL!"

With that, we fanned out onto the field, feeling the thick suburban grass beneath our cleats.

✳

Priding ourselves on being ghetto soccer stars, we Lowell ladies were guilty of some **affectation**. Lowell was the city's "nerd school," and we had the test scores and the **ponderous** backpacks to prove it. We resisted a **scholarly** image by hanging onto our city-girl attitudes. When Feibusch **mandated** us to get white shorts to wear on game days, some of us headed to Chinatown and bought red-and-white-striped underwear, which flashed **obscenely** through our **pellucid** shorts.

On the days we trekked out to the suburbs, miles away from our home turf, we tried even harder to **distinguish** ourselves from the **vapid** suburban girls. As we lined up

Muster: v. to summon up.
Guttural: adj. formed in the throat.
Affectation: n. artificiality of manner; pretension of qualities mot actually possessed.
Ponderous: adj. very heavy; hence, unwieldy; tedious.
Scholarly: adj. related to schools, scholars, or education.
Mandate: v. to command; require.
Obscene: adj. offensive to modest sensibilities; inappropriate.
Pellucid: adj. clear, limpid.
Distinguish: v. to mark, recognize, or see as distinct or different.
Vapid: adj. lacking liveliness, sharpness, or flavor; without life.

against this particular enemy team, the difference between our two teams was **comically apparent**. Our **motley** crew claimed an average height of five-foot-two and dressed in mismatched, loudly striped shorts. Meanwhile, more than half our opponents were blonde and they all wore flawless ponytails. From where I stood on the field, they seemed **homologous**. Several of the girls' faces were covered in makeup, the liquid foundation already bubbling with warm-up sweat.

I took my sweeper position back by the goal and watched as our respective team captains performed the pregame hand-shake. Even from across the field, I could tell how little the two girls wanted to participate in this **formality**. Their mutual **disdain** was that **palpable**.

Meanwhile, little Ngoc was facing down a blonde girl about twice her height. The girl had folded over the waist of her shorts so many times that her legs looked longer than a stork's. Across the field, Anamaria (our own leggy athlete) turned to our midfielder, cocked her head back toward one of the rivals and mouthed, "*Nose job!*"

This **confrontation** was starting to feel more like a show-down.

Chris was determined to make it even more interesting. She beckoned me back toward the goal.

"You know which one she is, right?"

Comical: adj. droll; funny; exciting mirth.
Apparent: adj. in plain view; clearly perceivable; obvious.
Motley: adj. composed of discordant elements; heterogeneous.
Homologous: adj. having the same relative position, proportion, or structure.
Formality: n. ceremony; a rule or procedure; perfunctory act.
Disdain: v. to look down upon; scorn; despise.
Palpable: adj. readily perceived; obvious; agreeable to the palate.
Confrontation: n. bring face to face with.

"Huh?" I didn't know what Chris was **alluding** to.

"The one you gotta take out." Chris pointed to the tall blonde. "Looks like a stork. You don't remember?"

I looked left and yanked my ponytail, **constricting** my hair more tightly. "Chris, I don't think I can . . ."

"*What*? You sent her flying last year!" Chris retorted. "Just be a little more graceful this time."

No wonder the Stork looked so familiar, I thought. How could I forget the sight of her long body flying through the air. Initially, I'd felt **contrite** about the collision. But when I looked down at my uniform and saw that her lipstick had smeared across my left sleeve, my sympathy quickly **evaporated**.

"I fell on my *butt* in front of her last year," I said to Chris. "You want me to do that again? I mean, revenge is cool and everything, but . . ."

"Whatever," Chris cut me off in her usual **peremptory** way. "You saw how she looked at you. She's asking for it."

I looked down the field. We were David's army facing off eleven beauty-queen Goliaths. Other than the **artillery** of insults in our mouths, we Lowell ladies had only one slingshot: my secret slide-tackle. Unfortunately, the secret to my slide-tackle was that I didn't know it.

The whistle blew and we were off, feeling **sanguine** and ready to sweat. Anamaria sprinted alongside Nose Job. Ngoc did her best to keep track of the Stork. I did my best to guard

---

Allude: v. to refer to casually or indirectly; reference.
Constrict: v. to cause to shrink; cramp; crush.
Contrite: adj. feeling remorse; repentant; expressing sorrow for a sin.
Evaporate: v. to disappear; dissipate.
Peremptory: adj. not allowing contradiction or refusal; dictatorial.
Artillery: n. all heavy mounted firearms.
Sanguine: adj. hopeful; confident; cheerful.

the goal. As sweeper, it was my job to **impede** any player who approached it. Meanwhile, I was terrified of tumbling to the ground in front of the Stork for the second year in a row.

But soon, that's precisely what I was doing. I not only tripped, but tripped just as the Stork and I were steps from the goal. She scored on me—twice.

"Goddamnit, Lauren, ya HESITATED!" yelled the 'Busch after the second goal, starting his usual **harangue**. "Get that finger out of your behind and DO SOMETHING with the goddamn ball!"

I **flushed** redder than the stripes on my underwear.

We did our best to remain **contenders**. By halftime, the home team was ahead 2–1. Feibusch paced on the sidelines, looking at the ground and shaking his head.

"You're lettin' 'em run all over ya," he **accused** us at half-time. "If you don't do the running in practice, how do you expect to do it here?"

Feibusch **heaved** a **dramatic** sigh as we sat around him, gulping water. "Gonzalez," he gestured to Anamaria with his chin. He could never quite pronounce her name. "*Left foot*, damnit!" He slapped his left thigh. "God gave you two feet for a reason! USE 'EM!"

Then came my turn. "Doctor Keane." Feibusch addressed me with this **moniker** to **mock** my overachievement in school.

Impede: v. to check or retard the progress of; hinder; obstruct.
Harangue: n. long vehement speech; a tirade.
Flush: v. to blush; glow.
Contenders: n. ones who compete.
Accuse: v. to charge with or blame.
Heave: v. to breathe laboriously.
Dramatic: adj. relating to drama: intensely interesting; eventful.
Moniker: n. a name or nickname.
Mock: v. to ridicule; deride; mimic.

He **monitored** all of our report cards to make sure we were working in the classroom as **assiduously** as we were on the field. "What, you're afraid to get her lipstick all over your shirt again? Whaddaya waiting for? GET IN THERE!"

I blushed again. Feibusch never passed up an opportunity to poke fun at me—whether it was for getting straight A's or **repudiating** makeup.

We quickly gulped down water and returned to the field like we owned it. Like a comeback was just ahead.

Anamaria led the way, netting a gorgeous goal. Jen took her momentum and scored soon after. But our burst of confidence was **evanescent**. As much as we hustled and elbowed, we couldn't keep up with Team Lipstick. None of us was used to playing on anything but hard-packed dirt. The **triad** of Lipstick, Nose Job, and the Stork **glided** effortlessly over the thick grass, picking up their feet in a perfectly **choreographed** ballet. We, on the other hand, might as well have been tromping through a tray of extra-creamy peanut butter.

As the game clock ticked away, the pressure for my "secret weapon" mounted. I could hear Chris **badgering** me from behind.

"Keanie! Three minutes to goooo!"

I **grimaced**, still not quite **amenable** to the idea of

Monitor: v. to keep track of.
Assiduous: adj. diligent; attentive; unremitting.
Repudiate: v. to refuse to accept.
Evanescent: adj. fades away, gradually disappears.
Triad: n. a group of three closely related things.
Glide: v. to move smoothly and easily.
Choreograph: v. to compose dances.
Badger: v. to pester; harass.
Grimace: n. a twisting of the face, expressive of pain, disgust.
Amenable: adj. agreeable; willing to cooperate or submit.

slide-tackling. The thing about the slide-tackle (even my **bastardized** version of it, in which I would sort of collapse one leg and pray that the other one would somehow find the ball) is that timing is everything. You have to know, from practicing it over and over again, **precisely** where your foot will meet the ball. In other words, before you do the tackling, you have to guesstimate how far you'll slide.

With two minutes left to play and my team behind by just one goal, I was huffing down the field with the **lithe** Stork, just barely keeping up. When she shifted her balance to shoot, I knew this was my last chance. If I let the Stork score, our defeat was guaranteed.

"NOW, DAMNIT, NOW! What the hell are you waiting for?" Feibusch yelled from the sidelines, trying to **impel** me to act.

I eyed the ball, **clenched** my jaw, and slid in for the kill.

Too soon! My brave leg slid way past the ball, missing its **trajectory** by at least two feet. On our rocky home turf, I would barely have slid six inches. But here, on the enemy's slick sod, I flew like a kid on a waterslide. The Stork pranced over my thigh and took her time winding up for a **magnificent** shot.

Chris was guarding the net and leapt toward the incoming ball with her fingers hyperextended. I watched, **paralyzed** on the plush grass, as Chris grabbed the ball midair. Save!

Chris kicked the ball downfield with all her strength, knowing our time was nearly out. We scrambled to advance

Bastardize: v. to debase; lower in worth, quality, or character.
Precise: adj. exactly defined; definite; accurate.
Lithe: adj. easily bent; pliant; flexible; supple.
Impel: v. to incite to action; urge.
Clench: v. to close tightly, as the fist or teeth.
Trajectory: n. the curve of a projectile in flight.
Magnificent: adj. great in size or extent.
Paralyzed: adj. helpless or unable to move; frozen.

toward the enemy goal, but it was **futile**. The whistle blew, sending us trotting back to our coach, **exhausted**. The final score was 3–2.

Feibusch was unusually **clement** with us, probably because we were like daughters to him. And he must have figured that our suburban losses had a **didactic** purpose, teaching us how to rise to the competition. We'd be back on the field the next day, with our usual **alacrity**.

"Get on home now, ladies. We'll pick things back up tomorrow."

He began walking to the parking lot when a freshman piped up, "Just wait till next year when they come play on *our* field."

Hearing this, Feibusch turned on his heel, energized **anew**.

"You gotta be *kidding*, these jokers'll *never* come into the city," he said, as if he'd rehearsed this harangue. "Why do you think we have to *haul* all the way out *here* every year? The city scares the *piss* out of 'em!" he declared with a **flourish**, spitting out the P and raising his bushy eyebrows for **emphasis**.

A giggle passed through our sweaty group. We turned to smirk at the **laureates**, as they loaded up the last of their **identical** sports gear and hopped into luxury cars.

Chris yanked up a small handful of suburb grass and held

Futile: adj. ineffective, idle; trifling.
Exhaust: v. to make empty or useless; tired.
Clement: adj. merciful; lenient.
Didactic: adj. instructive; expository; teaching.
Alacrity: n. cheerful willingness; promptness in response.
Anew: adv. once more; again; in a new form.
Flourish: v. to thrive; prosper.
Emphasis: n. stress laid upon anything; vigor or force in expression.
Laureate: n. recipient of honor or recognition for an achievement.
Identical: adj. the same; extremely close in resemblance.

the green divot in the air. "Think if we plant it back at school, it'll grow?" she asked with a mischievous grin.

Feibusch gently smacked her on the head with her goalie gloves. "Get on home, you jokers."

He turned to me with an afterthought before heading off the field.

"And you, Doctor Keane . . ."

I looked up from tying my shoes.

"Next year, you make sure you leave some lipstick on *her* shirt."

�֎ **Lauren Keane** grew up in San Francisco, California. She later moved to Connecticut to attend Yale and survived a total of five New England winters. She currently works at a Chinese-language magazine in Beijing and still plays soccer with a Chinese women's team. Lauren spends rare sunny afternoons wandering Beijing's back alleyways in search of people with stories to tell.

9

CONFESSIONS OF A HOMESCHOOLER

Timothy Michael Cooper

At the end of high school, all conversations seem to veer off in the same direction: toward college. Anything and everything you chat about with your friends—from the upcoming bio test to the rich kid who's getting a car for graduation—leads to the university. Everyone wants to know which schools you're applying to, whether you finished your essay, who's writing your recommendation, and how many hours away from Mom and Pop's you'd actually move. The college question is **inevitable** because the future is stressing out every member of your class. And every member in your class wants to make sure you're stressed out with them.

But imagine being pelted with the college questions if you had no **transcript**, no teachers, no test scores, and no GPA. Imagine if no student from your school had ever gone to college before.

Welcome to my life, six weeks before applications were due.

✳

Inevitable: adj. unavoidable.
Transcript: n. 1. an official copy of a student's educational record; 2. a typed copy of spoken material.

"So, you should really start looking at schools." My dad was trying to **incite** me to action again.

"Uh, I guess so," I replied **flippantly**, though I sensed my own **negligence**. I had been apathetic about applying all fall. My dad had started to list a few universities that he thought I should research. But his **paternal** wisdom had yet to light a fire under me.

I'd been thinking "about college" in the **abstract** way for a while. But from the safe **confines** of my kitchen, it was hard for me to consider actually living and studying in a new place. As the only student in my class, I wasn't under peer pressure to apply to the best colleges. And the fact that I had no guidance counselor didn't help matters. I was floating along in my pre-college bubble, because yes, I was homeschooled.

That's right: I never went to high school. I just stayed at home for four years and studied there. After years of explaining this to strangers, dentists, or mailmen startled to see me on a weekday, I had the homeschooling script practically memorized. Here's an **excerpt** from a **typical** conversation:

New Person: What high school do you go to?
Me: I don't go to a high school.
New Person: What, you got expelled?
Me: No, I'm homeschooled.
New Person: Your whole life?

Incite: v. to move to action; urge or stimulate.
Flippant: adj. disrespectful; treating serious things lightly.
Negligence: n. failure to exercise reasonable care; careless.
Paternal: adj. fatherly.
Abstract: adj. theoretical; not applied or practical; apart from concrete reality.
Confine: n. a boundary or border.
Excerpt: n. an extract from something written or printed.
Typical: adj. conforming to a type; being a representative specimen.

Me: No, just since seventh grade, after my family moved from California to upstate New York.

New Person: What, are you antisocial or something? Or are you just too smart for school?

Me: Neither. It just works for me.

New Person: Well, you must be lonely. I guess your parents made you do it, huh?

Me: Not really. The decision was mutual.

New Person: So you *are* too smart.

Me: Hey, would *you* turn down the chance to never go to school again?

New Person: Hmmmm . . .

Sometimes this conversation varied. But the variations were **minute**.

To prove that homeschooling has its perks, I might mention that my sister had **excluded** home ec. and **culinary** arts from the curriculum and took philosophy and religion instead. Other times I'd point out how homeschooling could be more efficient: you spend less time quieting down a big class, explaining homework assignments, and reviewing old concepts. Instead, you dive into new stuff, making the school day more **stimulating**.

If the person I was speaking with still looked skeptical of my **unorthodox** education, I would draw out the ace card of my pro-homeschooling **rhetoric**.

"I can wake up any time I want," I'd boast. It was true: As long as I logged in my daily study hours, I was not beholden to

Minute: adj. extremely small in size.
Exclude: v. to shut out; omit.
Culinary: adj. pertaining to cooking or the kitchen.
Stimulate: v. to incite to action; invigorate.
Unorthodox: adj. not approved or conventional; nontraditional.
Rhetoric: n. inflammatory language.

any alarm clock. And of course, since homeroom was, well, in my home, I never had to set foot on a yellow school bus again.

❋

"So, why don't we try visiting Boston this weekend?" My dad continued **lobbying** the idea of my, you know, applying to college on time. He was starting to sound **exasperated**.

I, on the other hand, was **nonchalant**. What was the hurry?

Then my dad kindly pointed out that I had four weeks left to figure out where I was applying, and to complete the applications.

That's when it dawned on me: If I didn't start filling out paperwork, I might live at home *forever*. And something told me that homeschool wouldn't be as fun beyond the teenage years.

So Boston it was. I agreed to make the trip with my dad. The Sox city was a **logical** start because we could first visit my dad's alma mater, MIT, along with some of the hundreds of other area colleges. I was pleasantly surprised to find that walking around college campuses was more fun than studying in my living room.

Since I didn't have to be back in class on Monday morning, my dad offered to detour our college trip through New Jersey and Pennsylvania. Over the next three weeks, I **immersed** myself in American colleges. Once on campus, I found it pretty **facile** to decide whether or not to apply to a given college. I either liked it or I didn't.

Lobby: v. to attempt to influence or sway (as a public official) toward a desired action.
Exasperate: v. to irritate extremely; annoy; make angry.
Nonchalant: adj. cool; having an air of easy indifference.
Logical: adj. reasonable; persuasive; to be expected; rational.
Immerse: v. to involve or interest deeply.
Facile: adj. easily accomplished or attained.

Once I had a list of prospective schools, it was time to fill out the application. I sat down newly **energized**. This was the easy part, right?

I began by **inscribing** my name and address.

Then I came to the name of my school. Huh. My school didn't really have a name. I was going to have to make something up. I decided to come back to that later. I wouldn't let this **hamper** my momentum. Next:

Attach a copy of your transcript.

Uh-oh.

"Dad, what are we going to do about my report card?" I asked.

"What do you mean?"

"Uh, I don't *have* a report card."

"Oh. Well, we're your teachers, so we'll make you one."

I was getting concerned. "Yeah, but what *grades* will you put on it?"

"You need grades?"

"Yes, I need grades!" I snapped, sounding **irritable**. How else would the admissions officers know how I did in any subject?

After consulting with my mom, my dad recognized the **quandary**. "Do you care what grades we give you?" he asked.

Tact **eluded** me. "Um, hello? What do you think?"

My parents were **ambivalent**, not knowing what was the

Energize: v. manifesting energy; vigorous in action; enthusiastic.
Inscribe: v. to write or engrave.
Hamper: v. to impede in motion or progress; hinder.
Irritable: adj. irascible; vexed; annoyed.
Quandary: n. state of bewilderment or perplexity; a dilemma.
Elude: v. to evade; avoid or escape by stratagem or deceit.
Ambivalent: adj. having mixed or conflicting feelings.

fair thing to do. They didn't want to **mete** out poor grades for the subjects I hadn't done as well in. However, the work and tests my parents gave me were more **rigorous** than the typical high school level. After much deliberation, my mom came to me with an answer. "We've decided to give you straight A's."

I held my tongue. On one hand, my parents' decision seemed **biased** in favor of homeschooling, while on the other hand, **indiscriminately** giving me poor grades made no more sense. I could just hear the comments of the admissions officers, *"This guy couldn't even get A's from his own parents!"*

Once the matter of grades was resolved, I went back to my application forms.

Now they wanted to know how I ranked among my classmates.

"Let's just leave this blank," my mom told me. "We don't want to be **deceitful**."

My dad felt otherwise. "This will cause the same problem as not giving him any grades—we need to make sure his ranking is somehow **comparable** to those of the other students."

This application process was turning into a disaster. Everything these colleges expected me to **furnish**—transcripts, teacher recommendations, state-exam scores, varsity letters—I didn't have. You can only **improvise** so much.

My parents were **shrewd** enough to fill in the "School

Mete: v. to give out by measure; dole.
Rigorous: adj. strict; austere; stern; harshly inflexible.
Bias: n. prejudice.
Indiscriminate: adj. not carefully selected; not discerning.
Deceitful: adj. tending to cheat; trick; delude.
Comparable: adj. similar; capable of being, or worthy to be, compared.
Furnish: v. to supply with what is needed.
Improvise: v. to make or do hastily or without previous preparation; extemporize.
Shrewd: adj. astute; quick-witted.

Ranking: ___ of ___," with the number 1 in both blanks. This wasn't **prevaricating**, they explained. I agreed, though I hoped no one would realize that I was not just first in my class, but also last.

As for the recommendation letters, my guidance counselor wrote me a glowing one. But I doubted it would escape the notice of the college admissions officers that this guidance counselor was dear old Mom.

❉

Homeschooling unfortunately didn't give me an excuse to slack in the essay section. I worked on my essays for hours on end, with many false starts. I figured the essay was my chance to explain the **oddities** of my educational background. I could lay out the pros and cons just like I did with the strangers at the supermarket or the carwash, but this time while using a lot of big words to awe the admissions counselors with my **verbosity**.

But I **plateaued** at the barrier everyone encounters: It is extremely difficult to write a **synopsis** of your entire life in a few hundred words. I went through dozens of drafts.

I wanted my essay to be normal, but to stand out in the pile. First, I attempted to write a brief play based on the questions people always ask homeschoolers. Then I decided to write an anecdote about a summer-camp counselor who had **influenced** me. I wasn't sure it was the most **phenomenal** essay of all time,

Prevaricate: v. to be evasive; lie.
Oddity: n. a strange person or thing.
Verbose: adj. using more words than are necessary; wordy.
Plateau: v. to reach a period or area of little change.
Synopsis: n. a summary; outline.
Influence: v. to control or affect others by authority.
Phenomenal: adj. notable; extraordinary; remarkable.

but it was good enough to drop in the mail. So I finally applied to college. My dad had never looked so relieved.

Not long after, I got a phone call. "This is Sarah from the admissions office," said the voice on the phone. "I have a question for you."

My stomach **turned**. I had clearly made an **egregious** error on the application. Were they going to **interrogate** me about getting all A's? Or question my class rank as #1? Could I blame it all on my parents?

"We were wondering," Sarah continued, "whether you scheduled your interview with any other schools yet."

I **recovered** my composure. "Um, no."

"Great. We want you to come here," she said.

"There?"

"See, we found your application very . . . *interesting* and think you should come here. Can you do it?"

I asked my dad if he'd drive me about two hours away for this **excursion**. Thrilled that I might actually move along to higher education, he said yes.

"Sure, I can come in," I told the admissions counselor, somewhat **anxiously**.

"Great, then we'll see you at 1:30."

❈

I was sitting in the admissions office, sweating, when Sarah came out to greet me. To my relief, she was only about four

Turn: v. to become sour; ferment.
Egregious: adj. extraordinarily flagrant; conspicuously bad.
Interrogate: v. to ask a question or questions.
Recover: v. to get or obtain (something lost) again; regain; save.
Excursion: n. a journey, usually for a specific purpose, and return to the starting point; a jaunt.
Anxious: adj. full of anxiety; worried.

years older than I was. Her informal **deportment** put me at ease.

"So, I noticed on your application that you were home-schooled. I've always wondered about people like you. Tell me: Do you get to wake up late every day?"

Who knew that homeschooling could prepare you for your admissions interview so well! This was *the* No. 1 question people always asked me. I could answer it in my sleep. The answer is: Of course. Absolutely. Every day is like a Saturday! Well, my actual response wasn't quite that **effervescent**.

"Yes," I started, "I do wake up late." She looked **invidious** for a second. I was going to have to **temper** my answer with **veracity**. ". . . But whether I wake up late or not, I still have to be **conscientious** and cover the same amount of class time I would at school. If I wake up at noon, I have to study past midnight. If I want to take a whole day off, for violin practice or an art project, I can do that, too."

She seemed satisfied. "What about if you're sick?"

"Tough. My mom makes me study in bed even when I'm **convalescent**."

"So there's no way to be absent, I guess."

"No. Though I tried once by driving to the local high school—just for kicks. But even then I was still in *a* school."

She laughed.

Apparently my honesty made me sound **objective**.

"And who taught you?"

Deportment: n. behavior; conduct.
Effervescent: adj. exhibiting excitement or liveliness; bubbly.
Invidious: adj. prompted by envy or ill will; calculated to offend.
Temper: v. to moderate; mitigate.
Veracity: n. truthfulness; accuracy.
Conscientious: adj. scrupulous; careful; meticulous.
Convalescent: adj. recovering gradually after sickness.
Objective: adj. free from personal prejudices; unbiased.

"I was lucky. My parents split the teaching. My dad teaches me math and science while my mom covers **literature**, history, and so on. But most of the time, I teach myself using **instructive** texts made for homeschoolers." Hey, it was good enough for Abraham Lincoln.

"But didn't living and studying in your home get kind of lonely?" Sarah wondered.

Ah, the **loneliness** issue. I was just as familiar with this question, but its answer was a bit more complicated than those of the others. Of course. Teenagers get lonely while surrounded by others, let alone their parents.

"Well, I do a lot of community activities," I began explaining. "I take private lessons in different sports, instruments, and languages, and attend some high school functions. So it isn't so bad."

The truth was I also spent an **immense** amount of time wishing I were with all my friends in school. And sometimes, yes, I felt angry. Though it's hard to distinguish **resentment** at your parents for limiting your social life from anger with the teachers who load you with homework. I decided that Sarah didn't need to know all of these **nuances**.

From Sarah's demeanor, I could tell she was interested in what I was saying. Her questions didn't sound the least bit **accusatory**. This put me at ease and made my thoughts became more **fluent**. Before I knew it, our interview had gone on for forty-five minutes longer than it was scheduled for. My dad,

Literature: n. artistic writings.
Instructive: adj. serving to teach or inform.
Loneliness: n. the quality or state of being alone.
Immense: adj. very large; huge; vast.
Resentment: n. injury or affront.
Nuance: n. a delicate degree or shade of difference.
Accusatory: adj. charging with guilt or blame.
Fluent: adj. facile in speech; voluble; smoothly flowing.

who had been waiting outside for the **duration**, took this as an **auspicious** sign.

"I guess they thought you were interesting," he said as we walked away.

❧

The waiting period is stressful for every college senior. But as I waited, I couldn't help thinking about the homeschooler's worst-case scenario: If all of my applications were rejected, I might be stuck with my parents *for the rest of my life.* This **frightful** possibility kept me up at night with a bad case of pre-acceptance **insomnia**.

My mom tried to **mitigate** my anxiety by promising that college applications were "a complete crapshoot." That was her way of explaining that the process was **capricious**. If the admissions counselor happened to read my application just before lunch, he might reject it just to get to his bologna sandwich more **expediently**. Or maybe the admissions officer who reviewed my application would have an ex-husband named Timothy and **discard** it for that **arbitrary** reason.

My fears only mounted.

The only thing that could **allay** my worries about the future

Duration: n. the length of time during which anything continues or lasts.
Auspicious: adj. well-omened; betokening success; favorable.
Frightful: adj. terrible; unpleasant.
Insomnia: n. inability to sleep, especially when chronic.
Mitigate: v. to lessen or decrease in severity.
Capricious: adj. fickle.
Expedient: adj. conducive to self-interest or a desired end.
Discard: v. to cast off; reject; throw away as useless.
Arbitrary: adj. not regulated by fixed rule or law; random.
Allay: v. to make quiet or calm; pacify.

was an acceptance letter with my name on it. I needed **finality**; I needed to see my future in writing. Fortunately (or unfortunately, for my mental health), since I was homeschooled, I could hang out and wait for the mailman at his regular hour. When he came one day carrying a **colossal** envelope, I hugged the guy.

❋

Now an adult, I'm happy to announce that I no longer live with my parents. I work as a writer in New York City, writing screenplays, restaurant reviews, and magazine articles. Since I'm considering going back to school for a graduate degree, I recently picked up a grad school application to **peruse**. After the section asking for "Name" and "Address", a few familiar questions appeared:

What is the name of your high school?
What was your GPA?
What was your class rank?

❋ **Timothy Michael Cooper** grew up in California and New York, attended high school at the prestigious "I Was Homeschooled" Academy located in his house, and went on to earn a B.A. in philosophy at Yale University. He now works as a playwright, screenwriter, humorist, and restaurant critic in Manhattan. He insists that people refer to him by all three of his names, which may be why he has never held a full-time job, and hopefully never will.

Finality: n. the character or condition of being settled, irrevocable, or complete.
Colossal: adj. huge; gigantic.
Peruse: v. to read through; look over.

10

CONFESSIONS OF A PIGSTY PRANKSTER

Dave Finney

My all-male school prided itself on turning its boys into bright young men. In my opinion, though, my high school **generated** bright young pranksters. Every spring, a new class of seniors graduated as experts in practical jokes. And every fall, a new class of freshmen arrived to play victims.

I'll never forget the first time I witnessed a master prank. I was sitting in study hall, doing my homework in that **assiduous** way a good little freshman does, when the door to the courtyard flew open. It was winter—the first snowfall of the year, in fact—and a cold wind rushed in to nip us. Before anyone knew what was happening, two big seniors reached in and dragged the nearest freshman straight out the door.

We leapt out of our seats to watch the rest through the window. We had to wipe away the fog for a **lucid** view.

"Gentlemen!" Our proctor barked at us to take our seats, but it was **futile**. Our poor classmate was **barreling** down the outside hill headfirst and we weren't about to miss it. The

Generate: v. to produce; form.
Assiduous: adj. diligent; attentive; unremitting.
Lucid: adj. clear; easily understood; distinct.
Futile: adj. ineffective or idle; trifling.
Barrel: v. to move at a high speed or without hesitation.

pranksters had turned him into a human sled. One of the guys sat **blithely** on his back, clutching his necktie like the reigns of a horse, while the other stood at the top of the hill and whooped. This was how freshmen at the Gilman School were **initiated**.

All winter long, whenever there was snow on the ground, upperclassmen would pop up around every locker alley and stairwell, to take you dashing through the snow, on a one frosh-open sleigh. And yes, they laughed all the way: ha, ha, ha. We freshmen were less amused by the winter joyrides. **Petrified** is a better word to describe our state. Between classes, when we were most **vulnerable**, we huddled together in the Freshman Locker Room and tried to figure out how we could get from the main hall to the science building without being **metamorphosed** into human toboggans. Our geometry lessons were actually **pertinent** in moments like these: *The closest distance between two points is a straight line.* We sprinted from history to biology like a misfit track team.

I was as scared as the next freshman, but I soon learned how to survive a long Gilman winter without **provoking** the older boys. If you "got sledded" early on—say, in November or December—the older boys tended to forget about you for the harsher months of January and February. It was like any **fraternal** hazing ritual: Everyone had to take a turn and, as best they could, take it well. The second part was important; if the

---

Blithe: adj. merry; joyous; glad.
Initiate: v. to set going; begin; start.
Petrify: v. to stupefy, as with fear; turn into stone; paralyze.
Vulnerable: adj. susceptible of being wounded, assaulted, or conquered.
Metamorphose: v. to change form, structure or appearance.
Pertinent: adj. to the point; appropriate; relevant.
Provoke: v. to incense; irritate; arouse; goad.
Fraternal: adj. brotherly

older boys gained some **deference** for you, they were less likely to **exploit** you the next time the **forecast** called for snow.

The teachers tried all sorts of **prohibitive** measures to keep us little freshmen safe. They locked **strategic** doors. They allowed us to gather in their classrooms long before the bell. They threatened the upperclassmen with demerits and **implemented** detention. The dean even **suspended** the senior privileges, like off-campus lunch, of a few especially **maverick** guys.

But no **intervention** could bring the freshman-sledding season to an end. Only once spring rain soaked the football field and turned it into a **hideous**, muddy slop did the Gilman Winter Olympics come to a close. With April ahead, the upperclassmen had something else on their minds. And no, I don't mean the girls at the school across the street. Far more **monumental** than prom, the first day of the month was April Fools' Day.

The senior class always took the lead on the April 1 pranks. It was their chance to make their mark at Gilman before **disbanding** and heading off to dozens of distant colleges. When I was a sophomore, a **cabal** of seniors **furtively** came to school

Deference: n. submission to the judgment of another; respect.
Exploit: v. to make use of; turn to one's own advantage.
Forecast: n. a prediction.
Prohibitive: adj. precluding or discouraging, as a high price.
Strategic: adj. of vital importance; using a careful plan or method.
Implement: v. to enact; execute.
Suspend: v. to postpone; stop temporarily.
Maverick: n. a dissenter; a nonconformist; an independent person not with a group.
Intervene: v. to intercede; interfere.
Hideous: adj. frightful in appearance or character.
Monumental: adj. imposing; notable.
Disband: v. to dissolve, as a band or group; dismiss, as troops from an army.
Cabal: n. a group of secret plotters.
Furtive: adj. sly; stealthy.

well before dawn and persuaded the security guard to open the school doors. The guard was happy to be **complicit** in the prank, snickering to himself as the seniors carried it out.

They dragged all of the desks out of the school building and lined them up on the football field. By the time we arrived for homeroom, the Gilman School was **devoid** of seating. The underclassmen stole by the windows to watch as the dean **marshaled** all of the seniors back out to the field. He then **enjoined** them to return every single seat to its rightful spot back inside, an **ordeal** that took the good part of an hour. Seeing as we spent the majority of our days glued in those wooden seats, **transcribing** algebra equations, the sight of our furniture laid out on the dewy grass was delightful. Much more delightful than, say, seeing our homeroom buddies made into bobsleds.

The April Fools' Day pranks held me in **awe**. The desk prank was **commendable** for its sheer scale. Watching from afar, we couldn't even count the number of **outcast** desks. By my standards, though, the desk scheme fell short of true prank perfection. The prank was not only **laborious** to do, but a bit **humiliating** to undo. The seniors were forced to lug all of the desks back into school in time for first period. This was the catch-22 of the senior prank: The bigger the spectacle, the bigger the cleanup. You could spend three years dreaming up the

Complicit: adj. the state of being an accomplice.
Devoid: adj. empty; destitute or lacking.
Marshal: v. to arrange in order; gather.
Enjoin: v. to command (a person) to do something.
Ordeal: n. a severe test; a trying experience.
Transcribe: v. to make a written copy of; to put into writing.
Awe: n. fear mingled with admiration or reverence.
Commendable: adj. praiseworthy.
Outcast: n. discarded matter.
Laborious: adj. not easy; requiring work.
Humiliate: v. to subject to shame or disgrace; mortify.

most **grandiose** scheme, only to end up with a mop in your hands on April Fools' Day.

This was exactly what happened to the boys in the grade above mine. They took the prank further than any class in Gilman history, making themselves **notorious** overnight. The prank had **transpired** by the time we arrived at school in the morning, but when we heard the **account** secondhand, we could imagine it perfectly.

The dean of students arrived at school early one morning. He passed by the hall calendar, not noticing that it was the first of April, and **proceeded** to his office. When the dean opened the door, a white **avalanche** fell around his feet. The entire room had been filled—it must have been four feet deep!—with Styrofoam packing peanuts.

To this day, I have no clue how the **intrepid** seniors pulled it off. Even if every member of their class had had the **foresight** to collect peanuts from all packages delivered to their homes—protecting their mothers' china and their fathers' power drills—they still couldn't have **accumulated** enough peanuts to fill that room.

The dean, finding himself chest-high in Styrofoam, tried to keep his **composure** but was obviously filled with **rancor**. He

Grandiose: adj. ostentatiously imposing.
Notorious: adj. widely but not favorably known; negatively famous.
Transpire: v. to happen; occur.
Account: n. explanatory statement; recital of facts.
Proceed: v. to go forward; continue or renew progress.
Avalanche: n. the sudden fall of a mass of ice and debris down the side of a mountain.
Intrepid: adj. undaunted; fearless.
Foresight: n. prudent care for the future.
Accumulate: v. collect or bring together; amass.
Composure: n. serenity; calmness.
Rancor: n. bitter animosity; spitefulness.

rounded up a handful of **culpable** seniors and made them scoop the white foam into trash bags. Even when the cleanup was complete and the dean could actually enter his office, the **remnants** crunched under his feet for weeks. Normally an **affable** guy, the dean **lapsed** into a truly **cantankerous** mood.

The rest of the Gilman student body got a **vicarious** thrill out of watching the seniors revolt. It was a kick for all of us. But, of course, it was impossible for us juniors to witness such a prank without trying to **divine** our own. We hoped to cause even more **upheaval** at Gilman. I often spent boring chemistry classes and **banal** study-hall periods daydreaming of a senior prank that would outdo all **precedents**. After all, a Gilman boy doesn't **endure** the winter sledding season like a champ without **devising** a few **stratagems** of his own.

❊

When senior year finally arrived, we were ready for it. OK, we weren't *quite* ready. There was still no **ingenious** prank, but

Culpable: adj. deserving censure; for being wrong, evil, or improper; blameworthy.

Remnant: n. a last trace; vestige.

Affable: adj. easy to approach; courteous; gracious.

Lapse: v. to decline; become less.

Cantankerous: adj. perverse in disposition; cross; ill-natured.

Vicarious: adj. substituting for, or feeling in place of, another.

Divine: v. to infer; discover by intuition or insight.

Upheaval: n. a violent disturbance, as a revolution.

Banal: adj. commonplace; usual.

Precedent: n. an identical or analogous previous example.

Endure: v. to bear with patience; put up with.

Devise: v. to think out; concoct; scheme.

Stratagem: n. a means of deception; a clever trick for gaining an end.

Ingenious: adj. showing cleverness in contrivance or construction.

we were using all of our **collective** mental muscle to **concoct** one. The basement locker room was our informal meeting space, where we passed extra minutes between class bells. Certain cool kids had **dominated** the locker-room conversation in the past, but now, as we neared that fateful April 1 box on the calendar, the **dynamic** was changing. Everyone—even kids who were usually **reserved**—started speaking up.

The same **laggard** who had just been dozing off in astronomy all of a sudden looked **animated** and shared a whole **litany** of ideas. Right beside him was a lanky artist, blathering on about his great vision: a **garish** paint job across our school's colonial façade. (In washable paint, borrowed from the first-graders, of course.) Seated to the left of this chatty Michelangelo was our beefy football lineman. He had a few pranks up his sleeve, too. When he laid his notebook open on his lap to show us, our mouths dropped open. The jock had **delineated** potential pranks in **tedious**, architect-style diagrams.

We were all becoming obsessed with April Fools' Day schemes, and I was no exception. Once I was elected to class council, I viewed our class's prank with extra **gravity**. Now I could actually organize my classmates. Granted, my official job

Collective: adj. combined; group.
Concoct: v. to devise; contrive, as a plot.
Dominate: v. to govern; control.
Dynamic: n. a surrounding force, especially political, social, or psychological.
Reserved: adj. reticent; self-restrained.
Laggard: n. one who falls behind; moves slowly.
Animated: adj. having life; lively.
Litany: n. a lengthy recitation; a sizeable series or set.
Garish: adj. showy; overdecorated.
Delineate: v. to mark the outline of; describe; depict; sketch.
Tedious: adj. long, slow, and tiresome.
Gravity: n. graveness.

was to put together **quotidian** events like mixers, pep rallies, and concerts. But I fantasized about more glamorous leadership—guiding them all, like some **exultant** general, in a prank that would earn the **adulation** of Gilman boys for years to come.

But a great leader needs great ideas. This was my **dilemma**. When I **officiated** at our locker-room summits, my brain quickly grew cluttered with other people's suggestions. Some proposals were just not **feasible** for a bunch of boys to **implement** in one day. Other ideas were too expensive. It was like playing on a football team with no coach and every guy trying to draw up the plays. Each day, the debate became more **fractious**.

I thought that the senior class's monthly "all-hands meeting" would finally be a chance to posit prank ideas in a more orderly fashion. While we normally had teachers moderating these meetings, it was Gilman policy that they also leave us alone for part of the meeting to allow "young men" to show their **mettle**. This was their idea of **fostering** leadership. To us, though, the teachers might as well have **condoned** our prank. As soon as they stepped out of the room, we changed the topic to April 1.

The meeting quickly turned into a **mobocracy**. People

Quotidian: adj. daily.
Exultant: adj. rejoicing.
Adulation: n. feigned devotion; excessive admiration.
Dilemma: n. a choice between alternatives equally undesirable.
Officiate: v. to act in an official capacity, esp. on some special occasion.
Feasible: adj. possible of realization.
Implement: v. to enact; execute.
Fractious: adj. unruly; quarrelsome; troublesome.
Mettle: n. natural temperament; courage.
Foster: v. to promote to growth or development of.
Condone: v. to allow; treat something as acceptable.
Mobocracy: n. rule by the mob.

began yelling and banging on desks. As soon as the teachers were gone, **contumacy** seemed to spread through the air.

"Order! Order!" yelled John, one of the other class officers, trying to **assert** some authority. "We've got some important business here, people."

But John didn't seem to have much **influence**. The **din** only got louder. Someone took a sandwich from his backpack and threw it across the room, where it splattered on a desk near another boy's head. Laughter followed.

But John was not about to lose control of the meeting. A former football player with grand plans of becoming a doctor, John was Harvard-bound. He tried **vociferating** more loudly.

"Come on! April Fools' Day is only a few weeks away!"

Now John had uttered the magic words. April: the month of fools. *Our* month! The room went quiet.

"How 'bout we go to the dean's house—real early—and jack up his Jeep!" one guy yelled **ardently**. "We could take the wheels somewhere and leave the car on cinder blocks!"

"But where would we put the wheels?" John asked, **challenging** the plot.

"We could **maroon** them on a goalpost. Let them dangle there like in a game of horseshoes," he **retorted**.

The class moaned. Of course it would be cool to put the

Contumacy: n. contempt of authority.
Assert: v. to claim and defend.
Influence: n. power to control or affect others by authority, persuasion, example.
Din: n. a continued clattering or ringing noise; a clamor.
Vociferate: v. to cry out noisily; shout.
Ardent: adj. fervent in feeling; intense; passionate.
Challenge: v. to demand explanation of; dispute as being incorrect.
Maroon: v. to abandon on a desolate island or coast; isolate.
Retort: v. to reply sharply.

wheels in a **conspicuous** place, but this would near on **larceny**.

"No, Einstein," John said. "That would require a crane."

"How about leaving the wheels up in the bell tower?" someone else tossed out.

But there was an obvious **impediment**. None of us had a key.

Discouraged, we started to fall back on more **conservative** schemes, like getting the entire senior class to walk out of school at **precisely** the same moment. A beautifully **synchronized** game of hooky.

"But then what?" John demanded. He was trying not to be **partisan**, but I could tell that he thought this was a **mediocre** idea.

"Maybe we could walk to our cars in one long **queue** and drive straight home?" offered one quiet boy.

"Or we could line up in some **formation** on the football field, spell something out maybe?" said another guy from the same **faction** of athletes.

People shouted out potential signatures:

"HAHA."

"FOOLS?"

"GOTCHA!"

Conspicuous: adj. easily seen; attracting attention.
Larceny: n. the wrongful taking of another's goods; theft.
Impediment: n. a load; hindrance.
Conservative: adj. moderate; not extreme; traditional.
Precise: adj. exactly defined; definite; accurate.
Synchronize: v. to agree in time; occur at the same time.
Partisan: adj. biased; adhering to a party or cause.
Mediocre: adj. of only moderate quality; ordinary; of lower ability.
Queue: n. a waiting line.
Formation: n. a formal structure of arrangement, esp. of troops.
Faction: n. a group or clique in a party, state, etc., seeking to promote partisan interests.

All three received a mix of boos and cheers.

Before we could even agree on the merits of Plan E, The Exodus, new ideas poured out. How about plastic wrap under all the toilet seats? Greasing doorknobs? Unscrewing lightbulbs? Clogging every single pencil sharpener with a wad of gum? Our class council was beginning to sound like a Three Stooges script.

"How about pi—" a small voice attempted to break in.

"Speak up," John invited.

Emboldened, the boy tried again, louder: "How about pigs?"

There were the snickers of **derision**, just as there had been after every new proposal. But then the **mocking** ceased. We went silent, **captivated**. I wondered what that Plan P would **entail**.

"I think we should buy some pigs, that's all."

This was Martin speaking. He was a latecomer to Gilman and few of us knew him well. He was a **laconic** guy. In fact, I'd never heard him say this much at all.

But it didn't take us long to decide that Martin was the **prophet** we'd been waiting for. *Pigs!* Pigs were **authentic**. Pigs were **preposterous**. And, most importantly, pigs were **unprecedented**. And that was what would really earn us

Embolden: v. to make bold; encourage.
Derision: n. act of deriding; ridicule.
Mock: v. to ridicule; deride; mimic.
Captivate: v. to enthrall; fascinate.
Entail: v. to involve as a consequence; cause to ensue; bring about.
Laconic: adj. using a minimum of words; concise.
Prophet: n. a spokesman, esp. one inspired by God.
Authentic: adj. genuine.
Preposterous: adj. absurd; contrary to common sense.
Unprecedented: adj. having no precedent; unexampled.

infamy: going where no Gilman boy had gone before. To the pig farm.

❊

As if the gods were smiling down on our prank, the timing was **auspicious**. The 4H Club auctioned off pigs every Wednesday night, and the first of April fell on a Thursday. I was at home the night before April Fools' Day, awaiting "the call." I was the **linchpin** of the operation; once Martin gave me the word, it would be time to set everyone else in motion. Around nine, I picked up the phone to hear Martin's voice, sounding urgent and **terse**. "We got 'em," was all he said.

From there, Plan P **unfolded**. John and I had **delegated** every piece of the prank to eager seniors, assigning some to buy the chicken wire, others to get hay, a few to pick up sawdust, and, lastly, one lucky guy to hunt down a trough. I trusted our helpers, but was still **apprehensive** about how it would all come together the next morning.

My nerves were buzzing as I approached the school building in the morning. I had come **prematurely**, unable to wait at home any longer. My cereal had gone soggy as I tapped my fingers against the breakfast room table.

The security guard had promised to unlock the school

Infamy: evil reputation brought about by something grossly criminal, shocking, or brutal.

Auspicious: adj. well-omened; betokening success.

Linchpin: n. something that holds together the elements of a complicated structure.

Terse: adj. saying much in a few words; concise; brusque.

Unfold: v. to reveal or become revealed.

Delegate: v. to entrust; empower.

Apprehensive: adj. uneasy or fearful about future events.

Premature: adj. happening before maturity or too soon; overhasty.

early that morning. Ever since he had gotten **entangled** in the Styrofoam stunt, April 1 had become his favorite day of the year, too. He didn't just quietly overlook our pranks, he **championed** them.

There was already a crowd at the front door when I reached it. Before I could **discern** anything through the doorway, a stench invaded by nostrils—a mix of hay, dirt, poop, and mischief. I didn't plug my nose. I was too **ecstatic**.

That's when I heard it: the first *oink*.

No way, I thought to myself. Did we really pull this off?

I pushed through the **horde** to see with my own eyes. Sure enough, there was a circular pig pen in the middle of our school lobby, clashing **obnoxiously** with the portraits of old men on the walls. What could be more **incompatible** with an **orthodox** prep school than an **odorous** pigsty?

The dean stood by, taking in the stench and the oinking. The teachers surrounded him, similarly **perplexed**, commenting to their **colleagues** in whispers. No one looked particularly furious, which I took to be a good sign. I wondered if our prank was so **absurd** that it might **transcend** punishment.

Entangle: v. to wrap or twist together; involve in a perplexing situation.
Champion: v. to defend; support.
Discern: v. to distinguish by the eye or the intellect; perceive.
Ecstatic: adj. having overpowering emotion or exaltation; rapturous.
Horde: n. a large troop or flock; a multitude.
Obnoxious: adj. odious; objectionable.
Incompatible: adj. unable to be harmonious together; not compatible.
Orthodox: adj. approved; conventional.
Odorous: adj. having an odor.
Perplex: v. to make confused or bewildered; puzzle.
Colleague: n. a professional associate.
Absurd: adj. contrary to common sense or sound judgment.
Transcend: v. to go or be beyond (a limit, etc.).

Sure, the dean looked a little **miffed**, but he also seemed somewhat **resigned** to the silliness of the situation.

The seniors slapped one another on the back in that too-cool-for-school, congratulatory way. Underclassmen gave us **extolling** glances, clearly regarding us as superheroes—like they owed us for the greatest laugh of their young lives. A couple of girls from the school across the street huddled in a corner and giggled.

As far as I'm concerned, our senior prank goes down in history. Some might **allege** that the Styrofoam-peanut gang had us beat, but their story ended with the **culprits** sweeping up their crime. Our tale has a more triumphant resolution. Rather than **discipline** us with poop-scooping the pigsty, our English teacher **intervened** and took the hogs back to his farm. Victory was ours. You could smell it in the air, all day long.

❋ **Dave Finney** grew up in Baltimore, Maryland. He attended Yale University, where he played on the varsity lacrosse team and wrote a column for the sports page of the newspaper. Since college, Dave has been a magazine editor, a web designer, a ski-lift operator, a waiter, and a novelist. He currently works in marketing and communications for an investment firm, far away from any farm animals.

Miff: v. to offend.
Resign: v. to submit oneself; be reconciled; endure with patience.
Extol: v. to praise highly; glorify.
Allege: v. to assert without proof or before proving.
Culprit: n. an offender; the guilty one.
Discipline: v. to train; chastise.
Intervene: v. to intercede; interfere.

GLOSSARY

Abate: v. to diminish; lessen.
Abduct: v. to carry off (as a person) by force.
Abet: v. to encourage; aid by approval, especially in bad conduct.
Abhor: v. to regard with extreme repugnance.
Abrade: v. to wear away by friction; roughen by rubbing.
Abreast: adv. alongside, side-by-side.
Abrupt: adj. sudden and unexpected.
Absolution: n. forgiveness of sins; remission of punishment for sins.
Absolve: v. to pardon; free from penalty.
Abstract: adj. theoretical; not applied or practical; apart from concrete reality.
Absurd: adj. contrary to common sense or sound judgment.
Abundant: adj. plentiful; present in great quantity.
Abysmal: adj. immeasurably low or wretched.
Accentuate: v. to stress; emphasize.
Accessible: adj. reachable; easy to communicate or deal with.
Accolade: n. a ceremony conferring honor, as knighthood.
Accompany: v. to go with; be associated with.
Accomplice: n. a partner in a crime.
Accord: v. to grant or give, especially as due or earned.
Account: n. explanatory statement; recital of facts.
Accrue: v. to accumulate or be added periodically.
Accumulate: v. collect or bring together; amass.
Accusatory: adj. charging with guilt or blame.
Accuse: v. to charge with or blame.
Acute: adj. having great perception or insight; sharp.

Adept: adj. skillful; expert.

Adequate: adj. sufficient; suitable.

Adhesion: n. steady or firm attachment.

Adjacent: adj. near or close, especially adjoining.

Adorn: v. to decorate; dress with ornaments; embellish.

Adroit: adj. expert in the use of hands or body; skillful; ingenious.

Adulation: n. feigned devotion; excessive admiration.

Adversaries: n. opponents in a contest; enemy.

Aesthetic: n. a particular theory or conception of beauty or art; a taste or approach to what is pleasing to the senses and the eye.

Affable: adj. easy to approach; courteous; gracious.

Affectation: n. artificiality of manner; pretension of qualities mot actually possessed

Affinity: n. an attraction to or liking for something.

Afoot: adv. adj. in the process of development; underway.

Agape: adj. with the mouth wide open.

Agenda: n. plan of things to be done; items of business.

Aggression: v. an act of hostility; an assault or encroachment.

Aghast: adj. filled with horror or shock.

Agitated: adj. nervous, anxious.

Agnostic: n. a person who believes that the existence of God is unknowable.

Agonize: v. to suffer anguish; to distress; put forth great effort.

Akimbo: adv. bent arms or legs, with the elbow or knee pointing outward.

Alacrity: n. cheerful willingness; promptness in response.

Albatross: n. a web-footed seabird of the petrel family.

Alien: adj. different in nature; foreign.

Alienate: v. to repel or turn away in feeling; estrange.

Allay: v. to make quiet or calm; pacify.

Allegation: n. an assertion without proof or before proving.

Allege: v. to assert without proof or before proving.

Allude: v. to refer casually or indirectly; reference.

Ally: n. one joined with another in a common enterprise; a confederate.

Aloof: adj. distant; removed; indifferent.

Altruistic: adj. unselfish regard for or devotion to the welfare of others.

Ambivalence: n. mixed or conflicting feelings.

Ambivalent: adj. having mixed or conflicting feelings.

Amble: v. move easily and gently, like a walking horse.

Ameliorate: v. to make better; improve.

Amenable: adj. agreeable; willing to cooperate or submit.

Amicable: adj. neighborly; friendly; showing goodwill.

Amorous: adj. inclined to love; loving.

Ample: adj. plentiful; sufficient.

Amusement: n. entertainment; pleasurable diversion.

Anarchy: n lack of government; a state of lawlessness.

Anathema: n. something or someone intensely disliked; a formal ban.

Anecdote: n. a short narrative of an occurrence; a story.

Anew: adv. once more; again; in a new form.

Animated: adj. lively, full of excitement and expression.

Animosity: n. ill will or resentment tending toward active hostility; an antagonistic attitude.

Annihilate: v. to destroy utterly; reduce to nothing.

Anonymity: n. lacking a name or identity.

Antic: n. attention-drawing behavior.

Anticipate: v. to expect; foresee.

Anxious: adj. full of anxiety; worried.

Apathy: n. lack of feeling; absence of emotion.

Aphorism: n. a short statement of a principle, often witty; an adage.

Apologetic: adj. expressing regret.

Apoplectic: adj. greatly excited or angered; causing a stroke.

Apparent: adj. in plain view; clearly perceivable; obvious.

Apprehension: n. anxiety or fear that something bad or unpleasant will happen.

Apprehensive: adj. uneasy or fearful about future events.

Approbation: n. approval, commendation.

Appropriate: adj. suitable; fitting for a particular purpose.

Aptitude: n. ability; innate talent for something.

Arbitrary: adj. not regulated by fixed rule or law; random.

Ardent: adj. fervent in feeling; intense; passionate.

Arid: adj. lacking moisture; parched with heat.

Aristocratic: adj. grand, stylish, and distinguished in manners.

Articulate: v. to say or speak distinctly, with clear separation of syllables.

Artillery: n. all heavy mounted firearms.

Artless: adj. without guile or deception.

Ascend: v. to climb up something, to rise or lead to a higher level.

Ascertain: v. to find out by examination; determine.

Asinine: adj. extremely stupid or foolish.

Assail: v. to attack violently with blows or words.

Assert: v. to claim and defend.

Assertive: adj. displaying confidence and self-esteem.

Assess: v. to estimate the value of.

Assiduous: adj. diligent; attentive; unremitting.

Assimilate: v. to take in and incorporate; absorb.

Assume: v. to take upon oneself; undertake.

Assure: v. to make sure or certain; make secure or stable.

Asylum: n. a place of refuge and protection; a secure retreat.

Atrocious: adj. appallingly bad; so ugly in taste or appearance as to revile.

Atrocity: n. an appalling, horrifying, or wicked state.

Atrophy: v. to waste away from lack of use or malnutrition.

Attest: v. to affirm to be true or genuine; to authenticate officially.

Attribute: v. to consider something as resulted by a cause; ascribe.

Aura: n. the atmosphere that surrounds a person or thing.

Auspicious: adj. well-omened; suggesting success; favorable.

Authentic: adj. actually of the ascribed authorship or origin; genuine.

Authentic: adj. genuine.

Authoritarian: adj. ruling by absolute authority.

Authoritative: adj. having due authority; showing an expectation of being obeyed.

Autonomy: n. self-governance; independence.

Avalanche: n. the sudden fall of a mass of ice and debris down the side of a mountain.

Awe: n. fear mingled with admiration or reverence.

Azure: adj. and n. sky blue.

Badger: v. to pester; harass.

Balk: v. to stop short and refuse to proceed.

Bamboozle: v. to deceive by underhanded methods.

Banal: adj. commonplace; usual.

Banish: v. to drive out or remove from a home or place.

Barely: adv. scarcely; hardly.

Barrel: v. to move at a high speed or without hesitation.

Bask: v. to take pleasure or derive enjoyment; lie in a pleasant atmosphere.

Bastardize: v. to debase; lower in worth, quality, or character.

Bawl: v. to shout clamorously; cry vehemently; wail.

Bedraggled: adj. unkempt; in a state of deterioration; untidy.

Behemoth: n. a huge, powerful person or animal.

Beleaguer: trouble; harass.

Beloved: adj. greatly loved; dear.

Bemoan: v. to express deep grief or distress over.

Bemused: adj. having feelings of tolerant amusement.
Beneficent: adj. doing or producing good; performing acts of charity.
Benign: adj. harmless, gentle.
Bequeath: v. to hand down; give or leave by will.
Bestow: v. to give; convey as a gift.
Bewilder: v. to confuse; perplex.
Bias: n. prejudice.
Bid: v. to command; invite; give expression to.
Bizarre: adj. odd; whimsical; grotesque.
Blatant: adj. obtrusive.
Blaze: v. to burn brightly; shine.
Blissful: adj. full of, marked by, or causing happiness.
Blithe: adj. merry; joyous; glad.
Bob: v. to move jerkily; go up and down quickly.
Boisterous: adj. noisy and violent; rowdy.
Bombard: v. to assail violently; attack.
Bombastic: adj. pompous; overblown.
Braggart: n. a boastful person.
Brandish: v. to wave (as a weapon) threateningly; to exhibit in an aggressive way.
Broadcast: v. to publish or spread widely.
Brood: v. to dwell gloomily on a subject; think about darkly, moodily.
Brusquely: adv. abruptly; curtly.
Budge: v. to move; stir.
Buffoon: n. someone who amuses others by clowning, by joking, or by ridiculous behavior.
Bulwark: n. a wall-like structure to keep out attackers.
Bungle: v. to cause something to fail through carelessness or incompetence.
Buoyant: adj. capable of floating.
Burgeon: v. to sprout buds.
Butt: n. someone or something that is an object of ridicule or contempt for other people.

Cabal: n. a group of secret plotters.
Cackle: v. to laugh especially in a harsh or sharp manner.
Cajole: v. to persuade by flattery, especially in the face of reluctance; gentle urging.
Calamity: an extraordinarily grave event marked by great loss and lasting distress; a great misfortune.

Callous: adj. being hardened and thickened; feeling no sympathy for others.

Candid: adj. outspoken; frank.

Candidate: n. one who seeks an office or honor.

Canonize: v. to designate as a saint; glorify.

Cantankerous: adj. perverse in disposition; cross; ill-natured.

Canter: n. trot or gait, often the three-beat gallop of a horse.

Capitulate: v. to surrender; give up.

Caprice: n. a whim; a sudden, impulsive action or notion.

Capricious: adj. fickle.

Captivate: v. to enthrall; fascinate; enchant.

Careen: v. to sway from side to side; to lurch.

Catalyst: n. the person or thing that sets off or causes an event.

Catapult: v. to throw or launch by or as if by a catapult.

Cathartic: adj. relating to purgation of the emotions.

Caustic: adj. severely critical or sarcastic; corrosive.

Cautiously: adv. warily; acting with fear.

Cerebral: adj. pertaining to the cerebrum or brain; intellectual.

Chagrin: n. mental disquiet or grief; self-dissatisfaction; distress or embarrassment at having failed.

Challenge: v. to demand explanation of; dispute as being unjust, invalid, or outmoded; confront.

Champion: v. to defend; support.

Channel: v. to transmit; send from one person or place to another.

Chaos: n. the absence of form or order; utter confusion.

Characteristic: adj. typical of a person, place or thing.

Charisma: n. a power for eliciting enthusiastic popular support attributed to a person or a position.

Chastise: v. to punish; especially corporally.

Cherish: v. to hold dear; treat with affection.

Cherubic: adj. an innocent-looking usually chubby and rosy person.

Chimera: n. an illusion of the imagination.

Choreograph: v. to compose dances.

Christen: v. to be given a name reflective of a quality or characteristic.

Churn: v. to agitate; experience violent motion.

Circuitous: adj. indirect, longer than the most direct route.

Circumscribe: v. to limit; bound; restrain within a boundary.

Circumspect: adj. careful of one's behavior; discreet.

Clamber: v. to climb awkwardly.

Clandestine: adj. secretive; surreptitious.

Clement: adj. merciful; lenient.
Clench: v. to close tightly, as the fist or teeth.
Clip: v. to cut, as with shears; truncate.
Clutch: v. to grab with the hands.
Coarse: adj. crude; unrefined.
Coerce: v. to compel by force.
Cognizant: adj. having knowledge of something especially through personal experience.
Cohort: n. a band, especially of warriors.
Collapse: v. to fall down suddenly, generally as a result of damage, structural weakness, or lack of support.
Colleague: n. a professional associate.
Collective: adj. combined; group.
Colossal: adj. huge; gigantic.
Comb: v. to search thoroughly.
Comely: adj. good-looking.
Comical: adj. droll; funny; exciting mirth; humorous.
Commemorative: adj. honoring or preserving the memory of.
Commence: v. to begin.
Commendable: adj. praiseworthy.
Commingle: v. to mingle together; blend.
Commute: v. to travel daily back and forth.
Comparable: adj. similar; capable of being, or worthy to be, compared.
Complacent: adj. self-satisfied.
Complaisant: adj. agreeable; compliant.
Complicit: adj. the state of being an accomplice.
Comply: v. to obey or conform to something, for example, a rule, law, wish or regulation.
Comport: v. to behave (oneself).
Composure: n. serenity; calmness.
Composure: n. serenity; calmness.
Compress: v. to pack tightly together; condense.
Comprise: v. to consist of, to be made up of.
Compunction: n. a slight regret or prick of conscience.
Concede: v. to admit or acknowledge something, often grudgingly or with reluctance; to surrender.
Conceive: v. to originate; cause to begin.
Concoct: v. to devise; contrive, as a plot.
Condone: v. to allow; treat something as acceptable.
Confidence: n. firm trust, reliance.

Confine: n. a boundary or border.

Confiscate: v. to take someone's property with authority, or appropriate it for personal use as if with authority.

Conformist: n. a person who adopts or accepts the usual standards or practices of a group without questioning them.

Confrontation: n. bring face to face with.

Conscientious: adj. careful; guided by conscience; principled.

Conscripted: adj. compulsory, required, obligatory.

Conservative: adj. moderate; not extreme; traditional.

Conspicuous: adj. easily seen; attracting attention.

Conspire: v. to agree together especially to do something wrong or illegal; plot secretly.

Constrict: v. cause to shrink; cramp; crush.

Contempt: n. the act of despising; a feeling of disdain.

Contenders: n. ones who compete.

Content: adj. satisfied; easy in mind.

Contented: adj. satisfied; placidly happy.

Contrite: adj. humbly penitent.

Contrive: v. to devise or bring about by clever planning.

Contumacy: n. contempt of authority.

Convalescent: adj. recovering gradually after sickness.

Convene: v. to assemble for some public purpose.

Convey: v. to communicate; impart.

Conviction: n. firmness of belief or opinion, or a belief of opinion that is held firmly.

Convivial: adj. festive; agreeable; jovial.

Convoluted: adj. too complex or intricate to understand easily.

Convulse: v. to jerk or shake violently and uncontrollably, sometimes with laughter or a strong emotion.

Copacetic: adj. satisfactory.

Coquette: n. a flirtatious woman.

Corps: n. a military force that carries out specialized duties, or a group of people who work together or are associated.

Corpulent: adj. bulky of body; stout; fat.

Corral: v. to pen up; enclose.

Corrode: v. to wear out or eat away gradually, especially by chemical action.

Courteous: adj. showing courtesy; polite.

Covert: adj. secret; hidden.

Cowardly: adj. Shrinking from pain or danger.

Cranium: n. the part of the skull containing the brain.
Credibility: n. the quality or power of inspiring belief.
Credible: adj. Worthy of belief; believable.
Crony: n. a close friend especially of long standing.
Crucial: adj. decisive; critical.
Crumble: v. to break into small pieces; disintegrate.
Culinary: adj. pertaining to cooking or the kitchen.
Culminate: v. to reach the highest point.
Culpable: adj. deserving censure for being wrong, evil, or improper; blameworthy.
Culprit: n. an offender; the guilty one.
Cultivate: v. to foster the growth of; promote the development of.
Cumulative: adj. increasing by accumulation.
Curable: adj. able to be remedied or corrected.
Cycle: n. a series or round.

Dabble: v. to do anything in a superficial manner.
Daunting: adj. tending to overwhelm or intimidate.
Debunk: v. to show the falseness of; expose as exaggerated.
Deceitful: adj. tending to cheat; trick; delude.
Decipher: v. to find the meaning of; decode.
Decisive: adj. final; conclusive; resolute.
Declamation: n. a speech of presentation spoken in a formal and theatrical style.
Decorum: n. propriety.
Decoy: n. one who allures as into a trap; anything used as a lure.
Deduce: to infer from a general principle; derive, as a conclusion.
Defective: adj. imperfect; broken.
Defensive: adj. protective; supportive in the face of criticism.
Deference: n. submission to the judgment of another; respect.
Deferential: adj. respectful.
Definitive: adj. conclusive; fixed; final.
Deft: adj. skillful; nimble; clever.
Degenerate: v. to deteriorate; sink into an inferior state.
Degrade: v. to demean; reduce to a lower rank; lower the dignity of.
Deify: v. to make a god of.
Deign: v. to do something in a way that shows it is a great favor and almost beneath dignity to do it; to stoop.
Dejected: adj. sad, depressed, dispirited.

Delectation: n. delight.

Delegate: v. to entrust to another; assign responsibility.

Deliberate: adj. intentional.

Delineate: v. to mark the outline of; describe; depict; sketch.

Delirious: adj. raving and confused.

Demolish: v. to destroy a building or other structure completely, or to beat an opponent very convincingly, especially in sports or debate.

Demolition: n. destruction; the instance of destroying.

Demonize: v. to equate a wicked or cruel person; turn into a demon.

Denouement: n. the solution of a plot in a play.

Denounce: v. to publicly declare something or someone wrong or evil.

Depart: v. to go or move away; leave.

Depiction: n. portrayal; representation by or as if by a picture.

Deplorable: adj. lamentable; calamitous.

Deploy: v. to more strategically or appropriately.

Deportment: n. behavior; conduct.

Deride: v. laugh at contemptuously; mock.

Derision: n. act of deriding; ridicule.

Desert: v. to abandon; forsake.

Designated: adj. one who is appointed.

Desist: v. to stop; forbear.

Desolate: adj. uninhabited; abandoned.

Desperate: adj. having lost hope; having an urgent need or desire; suffering extreme need or anxiety.

Despite: prep. notwithstanding; in spite of.

Despondent: adj. emotionally distant and removed, in low spirits.

Destruction: n. a scene of ruin.

Devilry: n. malicious mischief; wickedness.

Devise: v. to think out; concoct; scheme.

Devoid: adj. empty; destitute or lacking.

Devout: adj. devoted to, especially religion or religious worship.

Dexterity: n. ease and skill in physical movement, especially in using the hands and manipulating objects.

Diabolical: adj. connected with the devil or devil worship, or extremely cruel or evil.

Diaphanous: adj. transparent or translucent.

Diatribe: n. a bitter and abusive speech.

Dictate: v. to prescribe with authority; command.

Didactic: adj. instructive; expository; teaching.

Differential: n. a difference between two comparable values.

Dilapidated: adj. ruined, or fallen into partial or total ruin.

Dilemma: n. a problem involving a difficult choice; a choice between alternatives equally undesirable.

Dilettante: n. a person with interest in a hobby but no knowledge, commitment, or talent.

Diligent: adj. characterized by steady, earnest, and energetic effort.

Diminutive: adj. exceptionally or notably small.

Din: n. a loud, continued noise; a clamor.

Diplomacy: n. tact or skill in conducting any kind of negotiations; handling affairs without arousing hostility.

Disband: v. to dissolve, as a band or group; dismiss, as troops from an army.

Discard: v. to cast off; reject; throw away as useless.

Discern: v. to distinguish by the eye or intellect; perceive; discriminate.

Discipline: v. to train; chastise.

Discomfit: v. to embarrass; frustrate; disconcert.

Discountenance: n. disfavor; disapproval.

Discredit: v. to injure the reputation of; destroy confidence in.

Disdain: v. to look down upon; scorn; despise.

Disheveled: adj. untidy; unkempt.

Disingenuous: adj. lacking in candor; giving a false appearance.

Dismiss: v. to reject serious consideration of.

Dispel: v. to drive off or away; cause to vanish.

Displace: v. to put out of the usual or proper place.

Dissemble: v. to give a false impression about; conceal one's real motives.

Disseminate: v. to disperse throughout; scatter.

Dissimilar: adj. unlike.

Distinguish: v. to mark, recognize, or see as distinct or different.

Diverse: adj. essentially different; varied.

Diversity: n. variety; the state of being different.

Divine: v. to infer; discover by intuition or insight.

Divulge: v. to tell or make known previously secret information.

Dodge: v. to evade; avoid a duty or object.

Dole: v. to give or distribute as a charity; hand out.

Dolorous: adj. mournful; expressing or causing sorrow or pain.

Domain: n. a region marked by some physical feature.

Domestic: adj. relating to the household.

Dominate: v. to govern; control; hold control.

Don: v. to put on.

Donate: v. to make a gift or contribution.

Doppelgänger: n. someone who looks very like another person.

Douse: v. to plunge or submerge someone or something in water, or to put a lot of water or other liquid on someone or something.

Draconian: adj. harshly repressive; severe. (Origin: Draco, the writer of harsh ancient Greek laws.)

Dramatic: adj. relating to drama: intensely interesting; eventful.

Drastic: adj. having extreme and immediate effect; radical; harsh.

Drone: n. a monotonous, continuous sound, often buzzing, humming, or murmuring.

Drowsily: adv. sleepily.

Dubious: adj. doubting; unsettled in opinion.

Duplicity: n. bad faith; dissimulation; hypocrisy; double dealing.

Duration: n. the length of time during which anything continues or lasts.

Dynamic: n. a surrounding force, especially political, social, or psychological.

Ease: v. to lessen pressure; free from something.

Eccentric: adj. peculiar; irregular; deviating from the usual or recognized form; unconventional.

Ecstatic: adj. having overpowering emotion or exaltation; rapturous.

Edgy: adj. having a bold, provocative, or unconventional quality.

Edify: v. to instruct and improve, especially in moral and religious knowledge.

Effeminate: adj. marked by excessive delicacy; having traits traditionally considered feminine.

Effervescent: adj. exhibiting excitement or liveliness; bubbly.

Effusive: adj. expressive of great emotion.

Egregious: adj. extraordinarily flagrant; conspicuously bad.

Elated: adj. filled with extreme happiness and pride.

Elation: n. great joy; the quality or state of euphoria.

Elementary: adj. simple; pertaining to basic facts.

Elite: n. a superior or choice part, especially of a human society.

Eloquent: adj. having the power to speak vividly and appropriately; persuasive or expressive.

Elucidate: v. to make clear; explain.

Elude: v. to evade; avoid or escape by stratagem or deceit.

Elusive: adj. evading grasp or pursuit; cleverly avoiding.

Emaciated: adj. extremely thin or weak, usually because of illness or lack of food.

Embankment: n. a raised structure used especially to hold back water or to carry a roadway.

Embark: v. to set out; make a start.

Embellish: v. to heighten the attractiveness of by adding decorative details.

Embolden: v. to make bold; encourage.

Emerge: v. to appear; come into view from something that conceals, especially water.

Empathetic: adj. understanding and being sensitive to the feelings and experiences of others.

Empathize: v. to show sympathy for; to identify with or understand another's situation or feelings.

Emphasis: n. stress laid upon anything; vigor or force in expression.

Employ: v. to use; give occupation to.

Emulate: v. to strive to equal or excel; imitate with effort to surpass.

En masse: adj. all together; collectively.

Enamor: v. to enflame with love; charm; captivate.

Enchanted: adj. filled with delight and charm, as if cast under a spell.

Encore: n. a repeated performance, or additional act.

Endure: v. to bear with patience; put up with.

Energetic: adj. full of energy; operating with vigor; enthusiastic.

Engage: v. to involve; gain the attention of.

Engaging: adj. attracting of attention; intriguing.

Engross: v. to fully occupy.

Enigmatic: adj. mysterious; hard to understand; cryptic.

Enjoin: v. to command (a person) to do something.

Enlist: v. to enter, as a name on a list; enroll.

Enormity: n. the quality or state of being huge.

Ensconce: v. to establish; settle in.

Entail: v. to involve as a consequence; cause to ensue; bring about.

Entangle: v. to wrap or twist together; involve in a perplexing situation.

Enthrall: v. to captivate; charm.

Epaulet: n. a decoration on the shoulder of a jacket, especially on a military uniform.

Epic: adj. extending beyond the usual or ordinary, especially in size or scope.

Episode: n. an incident in a series of events; one happening.

Equanimity: n. evenness of mind or temper; calmness under stress.

Equivalent: adj. the same in magnitude, meaning, effect.

Erratic: adj. wandering; off course; lacking consistency.

Erudition: n. knowledge acquired through study and reading.

Escapade: n. a foolish or wild adventure.

Eschew: v. to keep away from; avoid.

Espy: v. to catch site of.

Euphonious: adj. having a pleasant sound.

Euphoria: n. a feeling of well-being or elation.

Evade: v. to escape from; avoid capture by; elude.

Evanescent: adj. fades away or gradually disappears.

Evaporate: v. to disappear; dissipate.

Evasion: n. the act of escaping; dodging something.

Eventual: adj. happening or to happen finally; ultimate.

Evict: v. to expel; kick out.

Exacerbate: v. to irritate; aggravate.

Exaggerate: v. to represent as large, important, etc., beyond the truth; magnify falsely.

Exasperate: v. to irritate extremely; annoy; make angry.

Exceptional: adj. unusual; extraordinary.

Excerpt: n. an extract from something written or printed.

Exclude: v. to shut out; omit.

Exculpate: v. to clear from a charge of fault or guilt; exonerate.

Excursion: n. a journey, usually for a specific purpose, and return to the starting point; a jaunt.

Execute: v. to do, perform, carry out.

Exhaust: v. to use up all that is available of something; make empty or useless.

Exhortation: n. language intended to incite and encourage.

Exonerate: v. to relieve of blame or accusation; exculpate; clear.

Expanse: n. an uninterrupted stretch or area.

Expedient: adj. conducive to self-interest or a desired end.

Expedite: v. to quicken the progress of.

Expedition: n. an excursion made by a group for a specific purpose.

Expenditure: n. an act of expending something; a spending.

Experiment: n. a trial or test.

Expertise: n. specialized skill or knowledge; know-how.

Explication: n. a clarification; an explanation.

Exploit: v. to make use of; turn to one's own advantage.

Exposition: n. speech or writing intended to explain or convey information.

Extemporaneous: adj. made, spoken, or performed without previous preparation; improvised at the moment.

Extenuate: v. to lessen the seriousness of; make light of.

Extol: v. to praise highly; glorify.

Extrapolate: v. to project on the basis of known data; infer.

Extravagance: n. an instance of excess; an excessive outlay of money.
Extricate: v. to free from something problematic.
Exuberant: adj. effusive in feeling or expression.
Exultant: adj. rejoicing; filled with great triumph.

Fabricate: v. to concoct falsely; invent.
Facile: adj. easily accomplished or attained.
Facilitate: v. to make easier.
Faction: n. a group or clique in a party, state, etc., seeking to promote partisan interests.
Falsetto: n. a very high voice, often used by male singers to sing high notes.
Fanatic: a zealot, especially in religion.
Fanfare: n. a flourish of trumpets; ceremony; ostentation.
Fare: n. 1. food served; 2. price charged to transport a person.
Fathom: v. to penetrate and come to understand.
Fatigue: n. weariness from physical or mental exertion.
Fatuous: adj. silly; foolish, especially in an unconscious way.
Faux: adj. imitation; artificial.
Fawn: v. to give exaggerated flattery or affection.
Faze: v. to ruffle; disturb the composure of; intimidate.
Feasible: adj. possible of realization.
Feat: n. an act of remarkable skill or valor.
Feign: v. to pretend.
Felicity: n. happiness; a source of happiness.
Felonious: adj. relating to crime or felony.
Feminine: adj. relating to, or like, woman.
Fervent: adj. with passion and intensity.
Festive: adj. joyous; relating to a feast or holiday.
Fiasco: n. a total failure.
Fidelity: n. faithfulness; loyalty.
Finale: n. a closing scene, especially of a musical performance.
Finality: n. the character or condition of being settled, irrevocable, or complete.
Fiscal: adj. pertaining to financial matters.
Flagrant: adj. outrageous; offensive.
Flail: v. to wave; swing.
Flash: v. to send forth suddenly.
Flaw: n. defect; imperfection.

Flippant: adj. disrespectful; treating serious things lightly.
Flourish: v. to thrive; prosper.
Fluent: adj. facile in speech; voluble; smoothly flowing.
Flush: v. to blush; glow.
Forecast: n. a prediction.
Foresee: v. to predict; anticipate.
Foresight: n. prudent care for the future.
Formal: adj. adhering to established form or mode; conventional; ceremonious.
Formality: n. ceremony; a rule or procedure; perfunctory act.
Formation: n. a formal structure of arrangement, especially of troops.
Formidable: adj. causing fear or apprehension; having qualities that discourage approach.
Fortuitous: adj. fortunate; lucky; happening by lucky chance.
Foster: v. to promote to growth or development of.
Fractious: adj. unruly; quarrelsome; troublesome.
Fracture: n. a breaking, especially of a bone.
Fragile: adj. easily broken; delicate; brittle.
Frantic: adj. frenzied; wild with excitement, pain or fear.
Fraternal: adj. brotherly.
Frenetic: adj. wildly excited or active.
Frequent: v. to go often or habitually go.
Frightful: adj. terrible; unpleasant.
Frigid: adj. chilly, in manner; formal.
Frolicsome: adj. merrymaking; fun.
Frustrate: v. to prevent from fulfilling plans, hopes, etc; balk; thwart.
Furious: adj. extremely angry.
Furnish: v. to supply with what is needed.
Furtive: adj. sly; stealthy.
Futile: adj. ineffective; serving no useful purpose; trifling.

Gaggle: n. a flock of geese, or a group of people, especially a noisy or disorderly group.
Gait: n. manner of walking, including pace and step.
Gargantuan: adj. enormous; gigantic.
Garish: adj. showy; overdecorated.
Garrulous: adj. excessively talkative, especially on trivial matters.
Gauche: adj. socially awkward.
Gaunt: adj. excessively thin and angular.
Gaze: v. to look at intently.

Generate: v. to produce; form.

Genial: adj. friendly, cheerful, pleasant.

Genteel: adj. elegantly graceful; having an upper-class or aristocratic manner or appearance.

Gesticulate: v. to make gestures to convey meaning.

Gesture: v. to move the head or limbs to convey emotion.

Glacial: adj. 1. moving or advancing extremely slowly; 2. pertaining to ice or glaciers.

Glee: n. mirth; delight.

Glide: v. to move smoothly and easily.

Gnarled: adj. full of knots; twisted into a state of deformity.

Gossamer: adj. light, delicate, or insubstantial.

Gossipmonger: n. a person who starts or spreads gossip.

Grandiose: adj. ostentatiously imposing.

Gratuitous: adj. freely given; unnecessary; being without cause.

Gravity: adj. serious behavior; solemnity.

Gregarious: adj. social; liking companionship.

Grimace: v. to twist the face in a way that expresses disgust or pain.

Grimy: adj. dirty.

Grovel: v. to crawl or be prone upon the earth; humble oneself.

Grueling: adj. exhausting; tiringly severe.

Guffaw: v. to laugh coarsely.

Guise: n. cloak; cover.

Guttural: adj. formed in the throat.

Habitual: adj. customary; by habit.

Hamper: v. to impede in motion or progress; hinder.

Haphazard: adj. occurring by chance; accidental; random

Harangue: n. long vehement speech; a tirade.

Harass: v. to annoy by repeated attacks; disturb or torment persistently.

Harrowing: adj. distressing; extremely disturbing.

Heartrending: adj. causing extreme grief, pity, or heartache.

Heave: v. to breathe laboriously.

Hedonistic: adj. living in pursuit of pleasure or self-gratification.

Heft: v. to heave; hoist.

Heist: v. to commit armed robbery on; steal.

Hesitant: adj. hesitating or prone to hesitation; undecided.

Hesitation: n. a falter or pause.

Hibernate: v. to be inactive or asleep; pass the winter in seclusion and resting, as bears and some animals do.

Hideous: adj. frightful in appearance or character.

Hoard: v. to amass; save; keep piling up.

Hobble: v. to limp; proceed haltingly.

Homogeneous: adj. of the same or similar kind.

Homologous: adj. having the same relative position, proportion, or structure.

Horde: n. a large troop or flock; a multitude.

Horrendous: adj. very unpleasant or terrible.

Humiliate: v. to subject to shame or disgrace; mortify.

Hurtle: v. to move at great speed, usually in a wildly uncontrolled manner.

Hustle: v. to go somewhere or do something fast or hurriedly; make haste.

Hyperbole: n. obvious exaggeration; an extravagant statement.

Iconoclast: n one who challenges cherished beliefs or traditional institutions.

Identical: adj. the same; extremely close in resemblance.

Idle: v. to operate while not connected; do nothing.

Idolize: v. to love or admire to excess; to worship as a god.

Illusion: n. a misleading image; something that deceives or misleads intellectually.

Illusory: adj. based on or producing an illusion; deceptive.

Imbibe: v. drink.

Immaculate: adj. perfectly clean; spotless.

Immense: adj. very large; huge; vast.

Immerse: v. to involve or interest deeply.

Impecunious: adj. without money; poor.

Impede: v. to check or retard the progress of; hinder; obstruct.

Impediment: n. a load; hindrance.

Impel: v. incite to action; urge.

Imperil: v. to put in danger; threaten.

Impersonation: n. assuming the character of another; imitation of another person's voice, mannerisms, etc.

Impetuous: adj. sudden and vehement in action; impulsive.

Implement: v. to enact; execute.

Implication: n. the conclusion or consequence of something; the resulting meaning.

Impotent: adj. lacking strength, power, or virility.

Impressionable: adj. easily influenced.

Improvise: v. to act or compose something, especially a sketch, play, song, or piece of music, without any preparation or set text to follow.

Improvise: v. to make or do hastily or without previous preparation; extemporize.

Inactive: adj. idle; sedentary; quiescent.

Inadvertent: adj. unintentional; accidental.

Inane: adj. void of sense or intelligence; silly.

Inaudible: adj. not able to be heard.

Incense: v. to excite to anger or resentment; enrage.

Incessant: adj. constant, continuing without pause or interruption.

Incident: n. an occurrence or event; a happening.

Incidental: adj. casual; minor.

Incisor: n. a front tooth typically adapted for cutting.

Incite: v. to move to action; urge or stimulate.

Incoherent: adj. noncomprehensible, illogical; lacking clarity.

Incompatible: adj. unable to be harmonious together; not compatible.

Incompetence: n. the lack of the necessary skills; the state of being unqualified.

Incompetent: adj. not fit or capable.

Incorrigible: adj. resistant to correction or reform; beyond reform.

Incredulous: adj. unwilling to admit or accept what is offered as true; expressing disbelief.

Incriminate: v. to show to be involved in a crime; charge; accuse.

Indecision: n. irresolution; lack of decision; wavering.

Indefinite: adj. having no fixed or specified limit; infinite.

Indelible: adj. not capable of being deleted or obliterated.

Indignant: adj. feeling or showing anger, especially righteous anger; resentful.

Indignity: n. an event that makes a person feel shame.

Indiscreet: adj. lacking in judgment.

Indiscriminate: adj. not carefully selected; not discerning.

Indolent: adj. lazy; sluggish.

Inefficiency: adj. the sate of being wasteful of time or energy.

Inept: adj. not apt, fit, or suited.

Inert: adj. having no power to move or act.

Inevitable: adj. unavoidable.

Infamous: adj. publicly known for an evil reputation or act; famous for negative reasons.

Infamy: n. evil reputation brought about by something grossly criminal, shocking, or brutal.

Infantile: adj. characteristic of a baby.

Infiltrate: v. to pass into or through.
Influence: n. power to control or affect others by authority, persuasion, example.
Influence: v. to control or affect others by authority.
Influx: n. a sudden arrival of a large number of people or things.
Infuriate: to make furious; enrage.
Ingenious: adj. showing cleverness in contrivance or construction.
Inherent: adj. belonging intrinsically; innate.
Initiate: v. to set going; begin; start.
Inkling: n. a hint.
Innate: adj. existing in one from birth; inborn.
Innocuous: adj. harmless.
Innovative: adj. introducing something new; novel.
Inordinate: adj. beyond proper limits; excessive.
Inquire: v. to ask about; seek knowledge (of).
Insatiable: adj. not satisfied.
Inscribe: v. to write or engrave.
Inscription: n. words or symbols written or carved into something, such as a book or monument.
Insecurity: n. self-doubt; something unstable.
Insidious: adj. subtle but with evil effect; seemingly harmless but actually damaging; harmful but enticing.
Insomnia: n. inability to sleep, especially when chronic.
Instigate: v. to urge or stimulate.
Instructive: adj. serving to teach or inform.
Insurgence: n, a rebellion or uprising against a government.
Insurmountable: adj. incapable of being overcome.
Insurrection: n. armed resistance to authority; a limited rebellion.
Intense: adj. existing in high degree; strong; acute.
Intention: n. purpose; aim.
Interlude: n. intervening time, period, or stage.
Interminably: adj. having or seeming to have no end.
Interrogate: v. to ask a question or questions.
Intersperse: v. to insert among other things.
Intervene: v. to intercede; interfere.
Intrepid: adj. undaunted; resolute; fearless.
Intrinsic: adj. being an innate or essential part; inherent.
Invective: n. an abusive speech; vituperation.
Inveterate: adj. firmly established or addicted by habit, custom, or usage.
Invidious: adj. prompted by envy or ill will; calculated to offend.
Invulnerable: adj. unable to be wounded, assaulted, or conquered.

Inwardly: adv. privately; secretly.

Iridescent: adj. glittering with changeable colors, like a rainbow.

Irk: v. to irritate; annoy.

Irreplaceable: adj. not replaceable.

Irresponsible: adj. not having or showing any care for the consequences of personal actions.

Irritable: adj. easily exasperated or annoyed.

Jabber: v. to talk rapidly in an incoherent way; chatter.

Jeopardize: v. to put someone or something at risk of being harmed or lost.

Jurisdiction: n. the power to make and enforce laws.

Juvenile: adj. young; youthful.

Labor: v. to work hard, particularly physical effort.

Laborious: adj. not easy; requiring much work or exertion.

Lackluster: adj. lacking energy, excitement, enthusiasm, or passion.

Laconic: adj. using a minimum of words; pithy.

Laggard: n. one who falls behind; moves slowly.

Lament: v. to express sorrow (for); mourn; bewail.

Languid: adj. slow and relaxed.

Lapse: v. to pass by or away gradually; end; become less.

Larceny: n. the wrongful taking of another's goods; theft.

Laureate: n. recipient of honor or recognition for an achievement.

Legend: n. 1. a person or thing who is well-known or famous in popular myth; 2. a story from the past.

Lexicon: n. a special vocabulary.

Liberate: v. to set free.

Lieu: n. place.

Likelihood: n. probability; expectancy.

Limber: adj. agile; flexible.

Limp: v. to walk favoring one leg; go unsteadily.

Linchpin: n. something that holds together the elements of a complicated structure.

Listless: adj. lacking energy or enthusiasm.

Litany: n. a sizeable series; a lengthy recitation.

Literature: n. artistic writings.

Lithe: adj. easily bent; pliant; flexible; supple.

Loathsome: adj. hateful.

Lob: v. to strike or toss something so that is moves slowly through the air in a high arc.

Lobby: v. to solicit the support of legislators; to try to influence the actions of.

Logical: adj. reasonable; persuasive; to be expected; rational.

Loiterer: n. someone who lingers idly.

Loneliness: n. the quality or state of being alone.

Loot: n. booty seized in war; plunder; spoils; something stolen.

Loquacious: adj. talkative.

Lore: n. knowledge about a particular subject.

Lough: n. a lake.

Lucid: adj. clear; easily understood; distinct.

Lumber: v. to move slowly, heavily, and awkwardly.

Luminous: adj. giving out light.

Lure: v. to entice.

Machismo: n. strong or aggressive masculine pride or behavior.

Maelstrom: n. a whirlpool; a tumultuous state of affairs.

Magnificent: adj. great in size or extent; splendid; brilliant.

Maintenance: n. the act of keeping and preserving equipment or property.

Malignant: adj. threatening danger; deadly or growing worse.

Malleable: adj. adaptable.

Mammoth: adj. gigantic; immense.

Mandate: v. to command.

Mania: n. a form of insanity, marking by great excitement.

Maniac: n. a person raving with madness.

Maniacal: adj. frenzied; excessively excited.

Manicure: v. to trim; polish; groom.

Manifest: adj. easily perceived; obvious; apparent.

Mantle: n. a role or position, especially one that can be passed from one person to another.

Mantra: n. a word or motto that embodies a principle; a repeated word or statement.

Maroon: v. to abandon on a desolate island or coast; isolate.

Marshal: v. to arrange in order; gather.

Martyr: n. a person who sacrifices something of great value and especially life itself for the sake of principle.

Marvel: v. to wonder at; be moved by wonder.

Mascot: n. an animal or person symbolizing a group.

Mass: n. a large or general assembly.

Massive: adj. bulky; heavy.

Materialize: v. to appear, to take physical form.

Matriarch: n. a woman having chief responsibility in a household.

Mauve: adj. a color or dye, moderate purple or lilac.

Maverick: n. a nonconformist; an independent person who does not go along with the group.

Maxim: n. short statement of a rule or truth; a proverbial saying.

Mayhem: n. a state of rowdy disorder.

Meander: v. to wander aimlessly, peruse a winding course.

Measured: adj. regulated by measure; deliberate; calculated.

Mecca: n. the holy city of Islam, goal of Muslim pilgrims; hence, a goal.

Mechanics: n. functional details or procedure.

Meddlesome: adj. disposed to interfering with what is not one's concern.

Mediocre: adj. of only moderate quality; ordinary; of lower ability.

Melancholy: adj. sad; pensive; depressed.

Melodrama: n. something having a sensational or theatrical quality.

Menace: adj. to post as a threat to.

Merciless: adj. pitiless; cruel; without mercy.

Merit: n. a commendable quality; worthiness; character or conduct deserving reward.

Metamorphose: v. to change form, structure or appearance.

Metamorphosis: n. a complete change or transformation.

Mete: v. to give out by measure; dole.

Meticulous: adj. careful.

Mettle: n. natural temperament; courage.

Microcosm: n. a miniature copy of something, especially when it represents or stands for a larger whole.

Miff: v. to offend.

Mighty: adj. powerful.

Migrate: v. to move periodically from one region to another.

Milestone: n. an important event in life.

Mimic: v. to imitate, especially derisively.

Miniature: n. something small of its kind.

Minion: n. a servile follower or underling; a subordinate person.

Minute: adj. extremely small in size.

Mischievous: adj. maliciously or playfully annoying.

Miscreant: n. a villain; a scoundrel.

Mishap: n. an unfortunate occurrence.

Missive: n. a letter or written communication.

Mite: n. a very small amount.

Mitigate: v. to lessen or decrease in severity.

Mobocracy: n. rule by the mob.

Mock: v. to ridicule; deride; mimic.

Momentous: adj. of great consequence; important.

Moniker: n. a name or nickname.

Monitor: v. to keep track of.

Monologue: n. a long talk by a single speaker.

Monomania: n. an exaggerated interest in one thing.

Monsoon: n. the seasonal wind, or the rainy season, of South Asia.

Monumental: adj. imposing; notable.

Morsel: n. a small piece or bit, especially of food.

Mortify: v. to humiliate.

Motley: adj. composed of diverse or discordant parts; a random assemblage.

Muddled: adj. confused or stupid.

Mundane: adj. ordinary; commonplace; usual.

Muse: v. to think or say reflectively.

Muster: v. to assemble, especially troops; to summon up.

Mythological: adj. lacking factual basis or historical validity.

Naïve: adj. unsophisticated; simplistic; unexposed to the world.

Nameless: adj. obscure; anonymous.

Narcissism: n. excessive concern for oneself.

Narration: n. story.

Narrative: n. a story.

Navigate: v. to sail or steer.

Negligence: n. failure to exercise reasonable care; careless.

Negligible: adj. of little importance.

Nemesis: n. a formidable rival or opponent.

Neophyte: n. a beginner; a novice.

Nominate: v. to propose, as a candidate.

Nonchalant: adj. full of disinterest; coolly unconcerned.

Nonchalantly: adv. coolly; without showing concern; indifferently.

Noncombatant: adj. not engaged in combat.

Noncommittal: adj. not committing oneself to a positive view or course.

Notify: v. to give attention to; inform.

Notion: n. a general idea; a somewhat vague belief.

Notoriety: n. the state of being known and talked of widely and unfavorably.

Notorious: adj. well-known for some undesirable feature or act.
Novelty: n. something new or unusual.
Novice: n. a person who is new to the circumstances in which he or she is placed.
Noxious: adj. physically harmful or destructive to living beings.
Nuance: n. a delicate degree or shade of difference.
Nuzzle: v. nestle; snuggle.

Obdurate: adj. resisting entreaty; hard-hearted.
Objective: adj. free from personal prejudices; unbiased.
Obligate: v. to require.
Oblivion: n. the state of being forgotten.
Oblivious: adj. unaware; lacking knowledge of.
Obnoxious: adj. odious; objectionable.
Obscene: adj. offensive to modest sensibilities.
Occlude: v. to shut in or out.
Oddity: n. a strange person or thing.
Odious: adj. hateful; repugnant.
Odorous: adj. having an odor.
Officiate: v. to act in an official capacity, esp. on some special occasion.
Officiate: v. to act in an official capacity; to administer the rules of a game or sport.
Officious: adj. acting unduly important; aggressive in offering unrequested help.
Ominous: adj. foretelling disaster; threatening.
Onslaught: n. a violent attack.
Onus: n. a burden; a charge.
Opponent: n. an adversary.
Opportune: adj. timely; appropriate.
Opportunist: n. one who is quick to grasp opportunities.
Opportunity: n. a favorable occasion or time.
Opprobrium: n. infamy; reproach.
Optimistic: adj. hopeful, confident and upbeat about the future.
Oration: n. a formal and dignified public speech.
Ordeal: n. a severe test; a trying experience.
Orgy: n. a period of indulgence in a particular activity or emotion, especially something that is disapproved of.
Origin: n. a source; a point of beginning.
Orthodox: adj. approved; conventional.

Ostentatious: adj. pretentiously displayed.
Outcast: n. discarded matter.
Outlandish: adj. unfamiliar; bizarre; odd.
Outstanding: adj. not paid or settled; remaining.
Overdose: n. an excessive dose, as of medicine.

P

Pact: n. an agreement.
Palatable: adj. tasty; acceptable.
Palatial: adj. grand, like a palace.
Palpable: adj. readily perceived; obvious; agreeable to the palate.
Parallel: adj. of lines or planes, never intersecting, equidistant at all
  points.
Paralyzed: adj. helpless or unable to move; frozen.
Parody: v. to imitate in a humorous manner; ridicule.
Partake: v. to participate; take part in.
Participate: v. to take part in something.
Partisan: adj. biased.
Paternal: adj. fatherly.
Patronize: v. to treat with condescension.
Paucity: n. smallness of quantity or number.
Peculiar: adj. odd; curious.
Pedantic: adj. relating to one who makes a show of knowledge.
Peer: n. an equal; match.
Pellucid: adj. clear, limpid.
Penitent: adj. repentant; feeling or expressing sorrow.
Perambulate: v. to walk about.
Peremptory: adj. not allowing contradiction or refusal; dictatorial.
Periodic: adj. recurring at regular intervals.
Perjury: n. the willful giving of false testimony.
Perpetrator: n. a person guilty of committing a crime.
Perpetual: adj. everlasting; continuous.
Perplex: v. to make confused or bewildered; puzzle.
Perplexed: adj. puzzled; baffled over the inability to understand.
Persevere: v. to persist in something.
Personify: v. to be the embodiment of; to represent as a person.
Perspire: v. to excrete waste fluids through the pores; sweat.
Pertinent: adj. to the point; appropriate; relevant.
Peruse: v. to examine or consider with attention and in detail.
Petrify: v. to turn into stone; or paralyze; stupefy, as with fear.
Phenomenal: adj. notable; extraordinary; remarkable.

Phrase: n. 1. a short, pithy expression; 2. a sequence of words that is not a sentence.

Philanthropic: of, or relating to aid.

Phrase: n. a short, pithy expression.

Physique: n. the structure and development of the body.

Picayune: adj. trifling; of little value.

Piece: n. fragment; a part or portion.

Pine: v. to yearn intensely and persistently especially for something unattainable.

Pique: v. to arouse the interest of.

Piteous: adj. Sad; arousing pity.

Pitiful: adj. deserving pity and sympathy.

Placate: v. to pacify; soothe.

Plateau: v. to reach a period or area of little change.

Plausible: adj. seemingly true or trustworthy.

Pleasurable: adj. pleasant; gratifying.

Plethora: n. an overfullness; superabundance.

Ploy: n. a game, an escapade or trick.

Plummet: v. to drop sharply and abruptly.

Ponder: v. to reflect (upon, over); consider deeply.

Ponderous: adj. very heavy; clumsy because of weight and size.

Pontificate: v. to speak about something in a knowing and pompous way, especially when not qualified to do so.

Portfolio: n. an itemized account.

Posse: n. a body of persons; a gang.

Potent: adj. powerful; strong; having authority.

Practicable: adj. capable of being done.

Precarious: adj. uncertain; insecure.

Precede: v. to go before in time, place, rank or importance.

Precedent: n. a person or thing that serves as a model.

Precipitous: adj. dangerously high or steep; sudden, without thought or warning.

Precise: adj. exactly defined; definite; accurate.

Precisely: adj. exactly defined; definite; accurate

Predatory: adj. preying upon others; acting with selfish motives.

Preferable: adj. having greater value or desirability.

Prelude: n. something preliminary or introductory.

Premature: adj. happening before maturity or too soon; overhasty.

Preoccupy: v. to take the attention of, to the exclusion of other matters.

Preposterous: adj. contrary to common sense; utterly absurd.

Prerogative: n. a special right, power, or privilege.

Prescient: adj. having foreknowledge; foresight.
Preternatural: adj. extraordinary; beyond what is natural.
Prevaricate: v. to be evasive; lie.
Prim: adj. stiffly formal.
Primary: adj. first; principal; of most importance.
Pristine: adj. original; unspoiled; fresh and clean as if new.
Privileged: adj. favored.
Proboscis: n. the human nose, especially when prominent.
Proceed: v. to go forward; continue or renew progress.
Proclaim: v. to declare publicly; announce officially.
Procure: v. to get possession of.
Proffer: v. to offer; put before a person for acceptance.
Profound: adj. thorough; complete; deep.
Prohibit: v. to forbid; to prevent.
Prohibitive: adj. tending to preclude or discourage, as a high price.
Prompt: adj. quick to act; performed immediately.
Propagate: v. to spread; disseminate.
Prophet: n. a spokesman, esp. one inspired by God.
Prospect: n. a possibility.
Prostrate: adj. lying flat; laid low.
Protest: v. to object or indicate disapproval.
Protomartyr: n. the first martyr in a cause or region.
Protrude: v. to stick out; project.
Provision: n. a measure taken beforehand to deal with a need or contingency.
Provisional: adj. conditional; temporary.
Provoke: v. to purposely prompt someone to response, usually to deliberately cause anger or annoyance.
Prowl: v. to roam about in search of something.
Proximity: n. nearness.
Prudence: n. discretion; foresight; careful judgment.
Prudent: adj. judicious; wise.
Psychedelic: adj. relating to hallucination (usually drug-induced).
Pugilism: n. boxing; the practice of fighting with the fists.
Pulse: v. to pulsate; throb.
Punctuate: v. to break into or interrupt at intervals.
Purgatory: n. a place or stat of temporary misery or suffering.
Putrid: adj. rotten; foul.
Puzzled: adj. perplexed; confused.

Quaint: adj. pleasingly or strikingly old-fashioned or unfamiliar.

Qualify: v. to fill the requirements for a place or occupation; to be fitted for something.

Quandary: n. a state of uncertainty about what to do.

Quarantine: n. a period of enforced seclusion.

Query: n. a question; an inquiry.

Queue: n. a waiting line.

Quibble: n. an evasive argument.

Quiescent: adj. inactive, latent and dormant.

Quiet: adj. composed, subdued, not loud.

Quip: n. a witty remark, especially one made on the spur of the moment.

Quirk: n. a peculiar trait.

Quizzical: adj. expressive of puzzlement, curiosity, or disbelief.

Quote: v. to repeat, copy or cite words previously uttered.

Quotidian: adj. daily; usual.

Racy: adj. lively, entertaining, and mildly sexually exciting.

Rambunctious: adj. boisterous; unruly.

Rancor: n. bitterness; hatred.

Random: adj. arbitrary, assorted by chance.

Rapidly: adv. quickly, speedily, happening in a short time.

Raspy: adj. harsh; grating.

Raucous: adj. making loud noise.

Rebellious: adj. defiant; resisting control.

Recapture: v. to take again; recover.

Reckless: adj. daring; imprudent; foolhardy.

Reclaim: v. to regain possession of.

Recline: v. to lean back.

Recoil: v. to spring back; react.

Reconcile: v. to restore to union and friendship; to settle differences.

Reconciliation: n. a restored union or friendship.

Recount: v. to tell; relate; narrate in order.

Recover: v. to get or obtain (something lost) again; regain; save.

Redeem: v. to perform or fulfill a promise.

Redundant: adj. excessive, especially using more words than are needed.

Refrain: v. to hold oneself back; abstain.

Refute: v. to defeat by argument or proof; disprove.

Regalia: n. emblems, insignia.

Reiterate: v. to repeat; say or do again.

Rejuvenate: v. to make youthful; renew; refresh.

Relate: v. to tell; narrate.

Relish: v. to be pleased with; appreciate.

Reluctant: adj. Acting or doing with positive disinclination; unwilling.

Remnant: n. a last trace; vestige.

Remonstrance: n. an objection; protest.

Remorse: n. self-accusatory regret.

Remote: adj. far away; distant; not closely connected.

Repress: v. to put down; subdue; crush.

Reprimand: v. to reprove severely; censure, esp. publicly.

Repudiate: v. to refuse to accept.

Repugnant: adj. highly distasteful; offensive.

Requisite: adj. required; necessary.

Resent: v. to be indignant at, as an insult; to show or feel displeasure from a sense of injury.

Resentment: n. injury or affront.

Reserved: adj. reticent; self-restrained.

Reside: v. to dwell or live in.

Resign: v. to submit oneself; be reconciled; endure with patience.

Resist: v. to withstand; oppose.

Resituate: v. to rearrange in a particular place.

Resolute: adj. determined and unwavering, steadfast.

Resonate: v. to have or produce resonance; vibrate.

Resurgent: adj. rising again; reviving.

Reticent: adj. keeping ones thoughts, feelings and personal affairs to oneself, restrained.

Retort: n. quick, witty, or sharp reply.

Retreat: v. to go back; run from an enemy.

Retrieve: v. to find again; recover; regain.

Reunite: v. to bring people together, or come together, after a separation.

Revelation: n. a striking accession of information.

Revelry: n. a boisterous merrymaking.

Reverberate: v. to reflect sound; continuously echo.

Reverently: adj. with awe and respect; worshipping.

Revert: v. to go back to a former place, position, or state; return.

Revoke: v. to repeal; cancel; take away.

Rhapsody: n. an expression of extravagant enthusiasm; a musical composition of irregular form.

Rhetoric: n. unnecessarily exaggerated or insincere speech or language; bombast.

Rhetorical: adj. asked merely for effect, with no answer expected.

Ribald: adj. coarsely humorous, using indecent humor.

Rigid: adj. stiff, unmoving.

Rigorous: adj. strict; austere; stern.

Ripplet: n. a small ripple.

Riveted: v. attracted or completely attentive.

Robust: adj. strong; vigorous.

Rookie: n. a new recruit, usually a first-year member of a sport or team.

Rotund: adj. round; plump.

Routine: adj. customary; habitual; ordinary.

Ruffian: n. a brutal man; thug.

Ruffian: n. someone who behaves in a rough, bullying, or violent way, often a member of a gang of criminal thugs.

Saccharine: adj. sweet; sugary.

Sage: n. profoundly wise person.

Salutary: adj. beneficial; caring.

Salvage: v. to save.

Sanguine: adj. hopeful; confident; cheerful.

Sapient: adj. wise.

Sarcastic: adj. being or using sarcasm; using sharp sartorial wit.

Sardonic: adj. sneering; sarcastic; cynical.

Satiate: v. to satisfy fully.

Saunter: v. to walk at an easy unhurried pace.

Savage: adj. fierce, violent and uncontrolled.

Savor: v. to enjoy something with unhurried appreciation.

Scamper: v. to run quickly and playfully.

Scheme: n. a regular or formal plan; a system.

Scheming: adj. skillful; nimble; clever.

Scholarly: adj. related to schools, scholars, or education.

Scoff: v. to express scorn, derision, or contempt; mock.

Scrutinize: v. to observe or investigate closely.

Sedate: adj. even-tempered; quiet and steady.

Seethe: v. to be agitated; suffer violent internal excitement.

Septuagenarian: n. a person between seventy and eighty years old.

Sequester: v. to put someone in an isolated or lonely place.

Seraph: n. an angel of the highest rank in the traditional medieval hierarchy of nine categories of angels.

Serendipity: n. an assumed talent for making discoveries by accident.

Serene: adj. calm, peaceful, tranquil.

Shabby: adj. much worn; run-down.

Shamble: v. slow shuffling.

Shrapnel: n. metal balls or fragment that are scattered when a shell bomb or bullet explodes.

Shrewd: adj. astute; quick-witted.

Shriek: n. shrill outcry or utterance.

Shriek: v. to utter a shrill cry.

Shroud: v. to cover, screen, or guard.

Shuffle: v. to move with scraping feet.

Sidelong: adj. directed to the side or slating to one side.

Siege: n. a prolonged effort to gain or overcome something.

Simultaneous: adj. existing, occurring or operating at the same time.

Singe: v. to burn slightly or superficially.

Sinister: adj. malicious; harmful; ominous.

Skate: v. to glide or roll.

Skeptical: adj. questioning or doubting, often of accepted opinions.

Skepticism: n. an attitude marked by a tendency to doubt what others accept to be true.

Skirt: v. to pass along the border of; go around in order to avoid.

Skittish: adj. nervous, restlessly active, jumpy.

Sleuth: v. to act as a detective; search for information.

Sneer: n. a scornful smirk, with one side of the lip raised; a mean smile.

Sole: adj. unique; only; alone.

Solidarity: n. unity based on common interests, objectives, and standards.

Solitary: adj. alone, solo, without others.

Somnolent: adj. sleepy; drowsy; tending to cause sleep.

Soporific: adj. causing sleep.

Sordid: adj. base; vile; dirty.

Souvenir: n. a token of remembrance.

Sovereign: adj. possessing extreme power.

Specialty: n. a special characteristic; a distinctive feature or quality.

Speculate: v. to meditate or ponder; reflect.

Spiteful: adj. full of petty spite; malicious.

Splayed: adj. spread out; turned outward; awkward.

Sprinting: v. to run at full speed.

Spurn: v. to reject with disdain.

Squall: v. to cry loudly and continuously, such as a child or injured animal.

Static: adj. fixed; stationary; stagnant.

Station: v. to assign; place.

Status quo: n. the existing state or condition.

Steadfast: adj. firm and unwavering, resolute.

Stealthily: adv. moving quietly and cautiously, to avoid being seen or heard.

Stealthy: adj. secret or furtive in action or character.

Steel: v. to instill with courage or resolution.

Stellar: adj. 1. outstanding; 2. relating to the stars.

Stimulate: v. to incite to action; invigorate.

Stoically: adv. enduring pain and hardship without showing feeling or complaining.

Steal: v. to go away from; to move secretly or unobserved.

Straightforward: adj. direct.

Stratagem: n. a means of deception; a trick.

Strategic: adj. of vital importance.

Strategy: n. a careful method or plan.

String: v. to hang.

Stupefy: v. to make stupid, groggy, or insensible; to astonish.

Stupor: n. state of extreme apathy; daze.

Stymied: adj. blocked by a minor but insurmountable obstacle.

Suave: adj. smooth in texture, performance, or style.

Submerge: v. to place or plunge underwater.

Subsist: v. to exist; remain alive.

Subtle: adj. quietly delicate; not obvious.

Succinct: adj. concise; brief.

Succumb: v. to give way under pressure; yield.

Sully: v. to stain; defile.

Summon: v. to rouse; call or send for, with authority.

Sumptuous: adj. lavish; luxurious; grand.

Superb: adj. magnificent; elegant; excellent.

Superficial: adj. not deep or thorough.

Superfluous: adj. more than is needed.

Superimpose: v. to place something over something else, usually so that both are still visible.

Supernatural: adj. or n. beyond what is natural; pertaining to a god or deity.

Supervise: v. to oversee; be in charge of.

Supine: adj. lying on the back.

Supplant: v. to displace and take the place of.

Supplement: v. to add to.

Supplication: n. a humble appeal to someone who has the power to grant a request.

Suppress: v. to restrain; abolish.

Survey: v. to view; scrutinize.

Suspend: v. to defer; postpone.

Sustain: v. to maintain; support; keep alive.

Swagger: v. to walk or behave with an arrogant confidence.

Swarm: v. to move or assemble in a crowd.

Swarthy: adj. with a dark and often weather-beaten complexion.

Swivel: v. to pivot; spin around.

Synchronize: v. to agree in time; occur at the same time.

Synopsis: n. a summary; outline.

Tacit: adj. understood or implied without being stated; implied but not expressed.

Taciturnity: n. silence; reservation in speaking.

Tactic: n. a method or device for accomplishing an end.

Talisman: n. an object held to act as a charm to bring good fortune.

Tangible: definite or concrete; capable of being identified.

Tedious: adj. long, slow, and tiresome.

Temper: v. to moderate; mitigate.

Temperate: adj. moderate.

Tentative: adj. not fully worked out or developed.

Terminate: v. to bring to an end; finish; conclude.

Territorial: adj. protecting a domain.

Terse: adj. saying much in few words.

Theorize: v. to form a theory about.

Thespian: n. an actor or actress.

Thrash: v. to hit hard repeatedly.

Threatened: v. to utter threats (against).

Throng: n. a crowding together of many persons; a pack of things pressed together.

Thwart: v. to prevent from accomplishing a purpose; frustrate; baffle.

Timbre: n. the character of a voice or sound.

Tireless: adj. diligent; untiring.

Tolerate: v. to bear with patience; to endure without complaint or ill effect.

Tout: v. to praise or publicize loudly or extravagantly; to describe boastfully.

Traction: n. the adhesive friction between a moving object and the surface on which it is moving.

Trajectory: n. the curve of a projectile in flight.

Tranquil: adj. calm; serene; undisturbed.

Transcend: v. to go or be beyond (a limit, etc.).

Transcribe: v. to make a written copy of; to put into writing.

Transcript: n. 1. an official copy of a student's educational record; 2. a typed copy of spoken material.

Transgress: v. to break or violate.

Transition: n. change from one place or state to another.

Transitory: adj. lasting only for a time; fleeting.

Transpire: v. to happen; occur.

Transport: v. carry from one place to another.

Traverse: v. to travel across or through.

Travesty: n. an exaggerated or absurd likeliness or imitation, a parody.

Treacherous: adj. unreliable; likely to betray trust.

Treachery: n. violation of allegiance or faith; betrayal of trust.

Treason: n. betrayal of trust.

Tremor: n. a shake, quiver or vibrations.

Tremulous: adj. trembling; unsteady.

Triad: n. a group of three closely related things.

Triumvirate: n. any group or set of three.

Trivial: adj. unimportant, of little value, minor.

Trot: v. to go at a brisk pace between a walk and a run.

Trounce: v. to defeat divisively; thrash.

Turn: v. to become sour; ferment.

Twitter: v. to giggle.

Typical: adj. conforming to a type; being a representative specimen.

Umbrageous: adj. spotted with shadows.

Unaccompanied: adj. without a companion, escort or partner; alone.

Unambiguous: adj. clear, with no uncertainty.

Unbecoming: adj. not attractive, fitting or appropriate.

Underling: n. one in a subordinate or inferior position.

Undeterred: adj. not discouraged or stopped.

Unfold: v. to reveal or become revealed.

Unify: v. to make into a single whole.

Unique: adj. being the only one of its kind; unusual; rare.

Unison: n. accord in sentiment or action.

Unorthodox: adj. not approved or conventional; nontraditional.
Unprecedented: adj. having no precedent; unexampled.
Unpredictable: adj. unable to foretell; unexpected.
Unruly: adj. not submissive; ungovernable; wild.
Upbraid: v. to blame; rebuke.
Upheaval: n. a violent disturbance, as a revolution.
Usher: v. to contribute to the beginning of; to conduct to a place like an usher.

Vacant: adj. empty; having no contents.
Vacuous: adj. mindless, empty, showing lack of content.
Valid: adj. well-grounded or justifiable.
Validate: v. to make valid; to confirm.
Validation: n. an act, process, or instance of confirming.
Valorous: adj. valiant; possessing courage or acting with bravery.
Vapid: adj. lacking liveliness, sharpness; without life.
Vassal: n. a slave; a subservient or subordinate person.
Velocity: n. quickness or rate of motion; speed.
Velvety: adj. something of similar texture to a fabric with a thick, soft pile.
Vengeance: n. retributive punishment; revenge.
Veracity: n. truthfulness; accuracy.
Verbose: adj. wordy; containing more words than necessary.
Veritable: adj. true; genuine.
Vernacular: n. pertaining to the native or common language of a place or group.
Version: n. a particular form or variant of something.
Versions: n. a particular form or variant of something.
Vicarious: adj. substituting for, or feeling in place of, another.
Vicariously: adv. Experiencing through the feelings or actions of another person.
Vigilance: n. being alert to detect danger.
Vigilantly: adj. alert and aware.
Vindicate: v. to free from accusation or blame.
Vindictive: adj. Disposed to seek revenge; bitter.
Violate: v. to break, or infringe, as a law or contract.
Visage: n. the face; the countenance, or look of a person.
Viscous: adj. sticky; thick.
Visible: adj. on view.
Visualize: v. to form a mental image of.

Vixen: n. a sexually attractive woman.
Vociferate: v. to cry out noisily; shout.
Vociferous: adj. exclaiming; clamorous; noisy.
Voluptuous: adj. suggesting sensual pleasure by fullness of form.
Voracious: adj. having a huge appetite; extremely eager.
Vulnerable: adj. susceptible to being assaulted or conquered; open to attack.

Waif: n. a stray animal or person.
Wane: v. to decrease, as in size; decline.
Wanton: adj. unrestrained, wild , reckless.
Wayward: adj. turning or changing irregularly.
Weathered: adj. conditioned by exposure.
Whang: v. to hit something and produce a loud resounding sound.
Whet: v. to excite; stimulate.
Whimper: v. to make a low whining sound.
Willowy: adj. slim, graceful, and elegant, partly because of being tall.
Wilt: v. to become or make limp or drooping.
Wily: adj. crafty; sly.
Wizened: adj. dried up; shriveled.
Wretched: adj. deeply distressed in body and mind; dejected.

Zealous: adj. earnest; ardently active; devoted.
Zenith: n. the highest point of anything; culmination.

ACKNOWLEDGMENTS

Thank you to the writers of this book—Tom, Chris, Dave, Lauren, Chris, Kara, Voop, and Timothy Michael Cooper— for having a sense of humor about their awkward years, and for working wonders with big, ponderous words. And special thanks to Judith Riven and Ali Bothwell for believing that word nerds like us could bring this book to life.

FOR THE BEST IN PAPERBACKS, LOOK FOR THE 🐧

In every corner of the world, on every subject under the sun, Penguin represents quality and variety—the very best in publishing today.

For complete information about books available from Penguin—including Penguin Classics, Penguin Compass, and Puffins—and how to order them, write to us at the appropriate address below. Please note that for copyright reasons the selection of books varies from country to country.

In the United States: Please write to *Penguin Group (USA), P.O. Box 12289 Dept. B, Newark, New Jersey 07101-5289* or call 1-800-788-6262.

In the United Kingdom: Please write to *Dept. EP, Penguin Books Ltd, Bath Road, Harmondsworth, West Drayton, Middlesex UB7 0DA.*

In Canada: Please write to *Penguin Books Canada Ltd, 90 Eglinton Avenue East, Suite 700, Toronto, Ontario M4P 2Y3.*

In Australia: Please write to *Penguin Books Australia Ltd, P.O. Box 257, Ringwood, Victoria 3134.*

In New Zealand: Please write to *Penguin Books (NZ) Ltd, Private Bag 102902, North Shore Mail Centre, Auckland 10.*

In India: Please write to *Penguin Books India Pvt Ltd, 11 Panchsheel Shopping Centre, Panchsheel Park, New Delhi 110 017.*

In the Netherlands: Please write to *Penguin Books Netherlands bv, Postbus 3507, NL-1001 AH Amsterdam.*

In Germany: Please write to *Penguin Books Deutschland GmbH, Metzlerstrasse 26, 60594 Frankfurt am Main.*

In Spain: Please write to *Penguin Books S. A., Bravo Murillo 19, 1° B, 28015 Madrid.*

In Italy: Please write to *Penguin Italia s.r.l., Via Benedetto Croce 2, 20094 Corsico, Milano.*

In France: Please write to *Penguin France, Le Carré Wilson, 62 rue Benjamin Baillaud, 31500 Toulouse.*

In Japan: Please write to *Penguin Books Japan Ltd, Kaneko Building, 2-3-25 Koraku, Bunkyo-Ku, Tokyo 112.*

In South Africa: Please write to *Penguin Books South Africa (Pty) Ltd, Private Bag X14, Parkview, 2122 Johannesburg.*